CONCLUSION: THE FUTURE OF LEADERSHIP AND
MANAGEMENT

REFERENCES

Dedication

To the resilient managers who stand at the heart of every organization, orchestrating its daily rhythms and ensuring its smooth function; to those who tirelessly ensure that the gears of industry and innovation mesh seamlessly, even when faced with constant change and challenges; to those who often work behind the scenes, their efforts often unnoticed but undeniably crucial; to those who dare to dream bigger, to see beyond the immediate horizon, and who aspire to ascend to executive roles not just for the title, but for the broader impact they wish to make:

This book is dedicated to you.

In your journey from management to executive leadership, you will traverse the spaces between, learning to balance the tactical with the strategic, the immediate with the visionary, and the individual with the collective. It is no easy path, but it is one filled with growth, discovery, and unparalleled potential.

May you find in these pages not just insights and knowledge, but also the inspiration to embrace the vast expanse of possibilities that lie ahead. To bridge the realms of management and leadership is to unlock a new dimension of influence, one where your actions resonate across the fabric of an organization and, ultimately, the world.

Here's to your journey, to the challenges you'll overcome, and to the leader you will become. Remember, every great executive once stood where you stand now. The path is yours to forge, and the future is waiting.

With utmost respect and admiration,

Thomas P Huber, PhD, MS ECS

Introduction: The Age-Old Debate

The sun rises, casting a golden hue over the skyscrapers of the business district. Within these towering structures, a plethora of decisions, strategies, and operations unfold daily. From the bustling start-up hub in Silicon Valley to the established boardrooms of Wall Street, two words resonate deeply: leadership and management. These terms, though distinct, form the backbone of organizational success, and their interplay holds the key to navigating the ever-evolving business landscape.

In the vast world of organizational dynamics, the dichotomy between leadership and management has been a topic of fervent discussion for decades. Scholars, business tycoons, and thought leaders have long debated the essence of these roles. Are they two sides of the same coin? Are they polar opposites? Or perhaps, do they exist on a continuum where one evolves into the other?

It's easy to get lost in the semantics, but this debate goes beyond mere words. The real crux lies in understanding the essence of these roles, the responsibilities they encompass, and the impact they have on an organization's trajectory. In a rapidly changing business environment, characterized by technological advancements, shifting consumer behaviors, and global interconnectedness, understanding the nuances between leadership and management has never been more crucial.

At its core, management often gravitates towards the tangible — the processes, systems, and structures that keep an organization running smoothly. It's about optimization, efficiency, and consistency. Managers, in their quintessential roles, ensure that the ship stays its course, even amidst turbulent waters.

On the other hand, leadership delves into the intangible realms of vision, inspiration, and change. Leaders don't just maintain the status quo; they challenge it. They're the torchbearers of innovation, the visionaries who see what's beyond the horizon and inspire others to journey alongside them.

In the modern corporate milieu, the lines between these roles blur. Today's managers are expected to be more than just process overseers; they're anticipated to inspire, motivate, and lead. Conversely, leaders are not just vision setters but are also expected to understand and sometimes immerse themselves in the day-to-day operations to drive their vision to fruition.

This book, "Leaders, Managers, and the Spaces Between: A Modern Guide," seeks to delve deep into this age-old debate, dissecting it with a contemporary lens. Through a blend of theoretical insights, real-world examples, and actionable strategies, we aim to provide clarity on this complex interplay.

As you turn the pages, you'll discover not just the differences between leadership and management, but also the symbiotic relationship they share. It's a journey that reveals how, when harmonized effectively, these roles can drive an organization to unparalleled heights.

So, whether you're an aspiring manager, an established leader, or someone navigating the intricate maze of corporate dynamics, this guide is your compass.

Chapter 1: Defining the Terms: What Do We Mean by Management and Leadership?

In our quest to understand the intricate dynamics of organizational success, we encounter two terms that seem to resonate with ubiquitous significance: management and leadership. These terms, often spoken in the same breath, stand as twin pillars supporting the edifice of any thriving enterprise. Yet, despite their apparent symbiosis, they are frequently misunderstood, misapplied, and even muddled together as if interchangeable.

In this critical chapter, we aim to dispel the fog surrounding these concepts by laying down precise definitions and boundaries for each term. We venture beyond mere dictionary meanings to explore the nuances that enrich our understanding of management and leadership, revealing the depth and complexity hidden within these deceptively simple labels. By doing so, we set the stage for a more detailed exploration of how these two roles intersect, diverge, and contribute to organizational excellence in subsequent chapters.

The task before us is not just academic. In today's fast-paced, interconnected world, where the stakes are high and margins for error ever-shrinking, a clear understanding of these terms is not a luxury—it's a necessity. Whether you're an aspiring manager, a seasoned leader, or someone interested in organizational behavior, clarity in these foundational concepts will equip you to navigate the complexities of modern business with greater confidence and competence.

So, as we turn the page to begin this exploration, we invite you to join us with an open mind. Be prepared to question conventional wisdom, to challenge your existing beliefs, and to emerge with a clearer, more nuanced understanding of two of the most vital roles in any organization: that of a manager and a leader. Through this journey, we hope to enrich your perspective, empowering you to contribute more effectively to your organization and to your own personal development.

Understanding the intricacies of management and leadership requires us first to address the common misconceptions that surround these terms. In many circles, especially outside the realm of academic or professional discourse, 'management' is simply seen as the act of overseeing tasks, while 'leadership' might be overly romanticized as the act of inspiring masses. Such interpretations, while not entirely wrong, are overly simplistic and fail to capture the depth and breadth of what these terms truly entail.

A Brief Introduction to the Terms

Tracing back through history, the concepts of management and leadership have rich tapestries that have been woven through time. The term 'management', derived from the Latin 'manus', meaning 'hand', originally pertained to the handling of a tool or a horse. Over time, as societies became more complex and organized, the term evolved. By the time of the industrial revolution, it took on a more structured form, referring to the orchestration of processes, people, and resources to achieve specific goals.

Management

Management, in its essence, pertains to the act of coordinating efforts to accomplish predetermined objectives. This coordination is achieved through the strategic application of resources, be it human, financial, technological, or physical. Management encompasses a wide range of activities, including planning, organizing, directing, and controlling an organization's operations.

Several elements are intrinsic to the concept of management:

- ☐ Control: Managers are tasked with ensuring that processes and activities stay within predefined parameters. This might mean overseeing financial budgets, ensuring that teams meet project timelines, or mitigating risks that might derail organizational objectives.
- ☐ Efficiency: At its core, management seeks to achieve the maximum output with the minimum input. Whether it's optimizing production lines in a factory or streamlining a software development process, the aim is always to improve efficiency.
- ☐ Processes: Management is deeply intertwined with the establishment and maintenance of processes. Well-defined processes ensure consistency, predictability, and reliability in operations.

In the realm of organizational hierarchy, managers are typically individuals who have been given the responsibility, either through position or delegation, to oversee specific functions, departments, or teams. They ensure that the work is done, goals are met, and resources are utilized effectively.

Leadership, on the other hand, has its origins in ancient civilizations. Leaders were often those who stood at the forefront, guiding tribes, communities, or entire nations. Whether it was in battle, during migrations, or in governing, leadership was about setting a vision and mobilizing people towards it. From the pharaohs of Egypt to the tribal chiefs of indigenous societies, leadership has always been about direction, inspiration, and, at times, transformation.

Leadership

Leadership, while encompassing some facets of management, is broader in scope and depth. Leadership is the ability to influence and guide individuals or groups to achieve a shared goal or vision.

It's less about processes and more about people; less about control and more about inspiration.

Key elements of leadership include:

- ☐ Inspiration: Leaders ignite passion and motivation. They inspire teams to go above and beyond, not because they have to, but because they want to.
- ☐ Vision: Leaders have a forward-looking perspective. They can visualize a future that might not yet exist and have the ability to communicate this vision in a way that resonates with others.
- ☐ Challenging the Status Quo: True leadership often involves thinking outside the box. Leaders are not afraid to challenge existing norms or paradigms in their pursuit of excellence or innovation.
- ☐ Empowerment: Leaders empower those around them. They create environments where individuals feel valued, heard, and motivated to take initiative.

In a broader sense, leadership is not confined to titles or positions. While CEOs, founders, or directors might naturally be perceived as leaders due to their roles, leadership can manifest at any level in an organization. A team lead, a project coordinator, or even an intern can exhibit leadership qualities by influencing and inspiring those around them.

Misinterpretations and Oversimplifications

The dynamics of management and leadership have been shaped by various stereotypes and misconceptions over time. While some of these perceptions may hint at the truth, they often overlook the multifaceted responsibilities and complexities intrinsic to both roles.

When one thinks of management, an image often conjured is that of a stern, clipboard-wielding individual, overseeing workers and ensuring tasks are carried out to the letter. This portrayal, frequently emphasized in media and pop culture, diminishes the rich tapestry of responsibilities a manager holds. Managers are not mere taskmasters; they are strategic thinkers who have to keep an eye on the bigger picture, anticipate challenges, and make decisions with far-reaching implications. They also play a pivotal role in team dynamics, recognizing individual strengths, addressing weaknesses, and fostering a cohesive team environment. Furthermore, the rapidly evolving corporate landscape requires managers to be continuous learners, updating their skills and adapting to new trends and technologies.

On the other side of the spectrum is leadership, often romanticized as the realm of charismatic trailblazers, individuals whose personalities alone can inspire and drive change. While charisma is undoubtedly an asset, leadership is a lot more nuanced. True leaders are both visionaries and grounded realists. They have the ability to visualize the future while understanding the practicalities and challenges of the present. Their strength lies not just in directing but in genuinely connecting with people, understanding their aspirations, fears, and motivations. Moreover, leadership isn't just about the highs; it's about resilience. Leaders navigate setbacks and challenges, recalibrating strategies and maintaining morale even in the face of adversity.

Adding another layer of complexity is the interwoven nature of modern organizational roles. Today's managers often find themselves donning the hats of leaders, especially in dynamic environments like startups. Conversely, leaders in established corporations may need to immerse themselves in operational details to effect meaningful change.

To truly understand and appreciate the domains of management and leadership, one must look beyond the stereotypes. It requires recognizing the depth, challenges, and opportunities that both roles present, ensuring a more comprehensive grasp of their importance in shaping the corporate world.

How the Meanings and Implications of Both Terms Have Evolved Over Time

The world of work and organizational structure has witnessed a transformational shift over the past century. Technological advancements, globalization, and the democratization of information have catalyzed these changes, impacting the very essence of what it means to manage and lead.

Management's Evolutionary Journey

In the earlier part of the 20th century, with the rise of the industrial era, organizations primarily valued efficiency and standardization. The assembly line methods championed by figures like Henry Ford epitomized this era. Management was about process optimization, and managers were akin to supervisors ensuring that the cogs in the machine ran smoothly.

As we transitioned into the latter half of the 20th century and early 21st century, the corporate world began to realize that efficiency alone was not a sustainable competitive advantage. With the digital revolution, markets became more volatile, competition fiercer, and innovation became the name of the game.

Management thus started encompassing more than just administration. Strategy and foresight became essential. Managers were no longer just supervisors; they were expected to anticipate market shifts, drive innovation, and make critical decisions that could pivot the company's direction. The rise of concepts like 'intrapreneurship' highlighted this shift, where managers within large organizations were encouraged to think like entrepreneurs, identifying new opportunities and driving innovation.

This transformation in management's role reflects broader changes in the business environment. The shift was partly fueled by advances in technology and communication. Where managers were once primarily focused on internal operations, the global reach enabled by the internet and digital technologies has expanded the scope of their responsibilities to include a wide array of external factors such as global supply chains, offshoring, and the complexities that come with managing a geographically dispersed workforce.

Feeding into this shift was a change in consumer expectations. The modern consumer is more informed and has greater choices than ever before. They expect customization, rapid response, and high quality. Meeting these expectations requires a level of agility and customer focus that the old assembly-line model of management simply can't provide. It's not just about producing a product or service as efficiently as possible; it's about producing something that someone actually wants, and quickly adapting as those wants change.

The challenges posed by social and environmental considerations have made management more complex but also more critical. Issues such as sustainability, corporate social responsibility, and ethical governance have forced managers to consider not just profitability, but also the broader impact of their decisions on the community and the environment.

These changes have also affected the skill sets required of effective managers. Adeptness in technologies like data analytics tools, customer relationship management software, and other digital platforms has become indispensable. Emotional intelligence, cross-cultural awareness, and the ability to manage diversity are increasingly valued skills, reflecting a broader shift from the 'command and control' model to a more consultative and inclusive style of management.

We now see a more holistic form of management that marries the administrative skills of the past with the strategic vision, emotional intelligence, and technological proficiency needed for the future. Managers are now expected to be leaders as well, guiding their teams through uncertain environments with an eye on long-term goals while attending to the immediate needs of the day.

This evolution of management is a fascinating journey, one that underscores its adaptability and resilience as a discipline. It's a shift that recognizes that people, technology, and strategy are not separate realms, but interconnected gears in the complex machinery that drives modern business. And as we look to the future, it's clear that the role of management will continue to evolve, shaped by technological advancements, social changes, and the ever-present drive to find new and better ways of doing things.

Leadership: From Hierarchies to Networks

The early perception of leadership was heavily tied to authority, hierarchy, and charisma. Leaders were often seen as figures at the pinnacle of organizations — individuals with an almost magnetic charm, capable of rallying masses behind them. Their words were often taken as gospel, and dissent was rarely encouraged.

The latter half of the 20th century began challenging these traditional notions. The civil rights movement, the feminist movement, and other socio-cultural revolutions played a role in democratizing the concept of leadership. It was no longer solely about authoritative figures at the top but about influence, regardless of one's position in the hierarchy.

The advent of the information age further accelerated this shift. As organizations flattened and team dynamics changed, leadership began to be recognized at all levels. Team leads, project managers, and even individual contributors could exhibit leadership by influencing outcomes, fostering collaboration, and driving change.

In today's interconnected and networked world, leadership is also about building and nurturing relationships. It's about fostering a culture where every team member feels empowered to voice their opinions, take initiative, and contribute to the broader vision. As John Quincy Adams aptly put, it's about inspiring others to dream more, learn more, and become more.

This democratization of leadership dovetails with the rise of more collaborative organizational structures. Gone are the days when leadership was confined to the C-suite. Today, it permeates throughout an organization, from frontline employees all the way to the top. The decentralization of decision-making enabled by digital tools and platforms allows for quicker, more flexible responses to challenges and opportunities. In this context, the leader's role is not so much to dictate actions but to set the stage for innovation and enable team members to execute visions effectively.

The emergence of global networks and cross-functional teams has further complicated yet enriched the tapestry of leadership. Now, more than ever, leaders need to understand the nuances of cross-cultural communication, managing not just across departments but across time zones and national boundaries. Leaders are now connectors, bridging various stakeholders like employees, clients, and shareholders to create synergies and mutual understanding.

The transformation from hierarchical to networked leadership also brings about a different skill set. Emotional intelligence, strategic foresight, and adaptability become more crucial than ever. The ability to inspire and bring out the best in others takes precedence over autocratic decision-making. An effective modern leader is often described as a 'servant leader,' one who leads by serving others, meeting their teams' needs to enhance performance and well-being.

The concept of 'distributed leadership' also gains traction in this era of networks. Distributed leadership suggests that the task of leading can be shared among multiple individuals rather than residing in a single charismatic figure. This form of leadership recognizes the various strengths and capabilities across a team and leverages them for the benefit of the organization.

The shift to networked leadership also has implications for how we develop leaders. Training programs are moving beyond traditional management skills to include lessons in collaboration, conflict resolution, and even mindfulness. Executive coaching and mentorship now often focus on how to be an effective leader in a decentralized, networked context, emphasizing the importance of soft skills like empathy and listening.

Importantly, this shift also has a significant impact on diversity and inclusion. The networked model of leadership is inherently more inclusive, allowing people from various backgrounds, with different skill sets, to take on leadership roles. The authoritarian model often favored those who fit a particular mold, but today's complex challenges require a variety of perspectives and skills, making diversity a business imperative rather than just a social one.

As we navigate the complexities of the 21st century, it's clear that the model of leadership is continuously evolving to meet the demands of a rapidly changing world. The future of leadership will likely be even more distributed, more reliant on soft skills, and more inclusive than it is today. And just like its counterpart—management—leadership will continue to adapt, proving its resilience and relevance in shaping not just organizations but society at large.

Convergence of Roles

The contemporary business environment, marked by rapid technological advancements, globalization, and shifting organizational paradigms, has necessitated a reevaluation of traditional roles within enterprises. As the boundaries of industries blur and new challenges arise, so too have the lines between management and leadership begun to merge. This convergence is more than just an overlap; it's a symbiotic evolution that acknowledges the strengths of both roles and blends them for the benefit of modern organizations.

Historically, managers were primarily seen as the custodians of processes. They ensured that tasks were completed, resources were allocated efficiently, and goals were met. Their domain was the tangible, the measurable, the day-to-day. Leadership, on the other hand, dwelt in the intangible. Leaders were the visionaries, those who inspired, who dreamt big, and who charted the course for the future. They were the motivators, the change agents, the disruptors.

As businesses faced an increasingly volatile, uncertain, complex, and ambiguous (often referred to as VUCA) world, it became evident that these siloed roles were insufficient. Organizations needed managers who could inspire and lead, and leaders who understood the intricacies of operations and could execute their visions effectively.

Today's managers are no longer confined to mere operational oversight. They're being called upon to be more proactive, to anticipate market shifts, to innovate, and most importantly, to inspire their teams. A manager in a modern organization is not just monitoring performance metrics but is also shaping the culture, fostering collaboration, and ensuring that team members are aligned with the company's vision and values. This shift demands that they embody many of the traits traditionally associated with leaders — from visionary thinking to empathy.

Leaders are finding that vision without execution is futile. A grand strategy, if not grounded in operational reality, risks becoming a mere pipe dream. Hence, effective leaders of today are immersing themselves in the nitty-gritty of their organizations. They are collaborating closely with their teams, understanding challenges at the ground level, and leveraging management principles to ensure their visions are translated into actionable, achievable plans.

This convergence is also reflected in organizational structures. Hierarchical, top-down structures are giving way to more agile, team-based models. Here, leadership is distributed, and managerial roles are fluid. A project lead today might be a team member tomorrow, and leadership is often situational, based on expertise and need rather than title.

The modern business landscape requires professionals who can seamlessly blend the strategic foresight of leadership with the tactical precision of management. This convergence of roles ensures that organizations remain agile, resilient, and equipped to navigate the complexities of the 21st century.

The convergence of roles between leadership and management is not just a trend but a significant paradigm shift that addresses the complex demands of today's business environment. In an age where adaptability and agility are not just desirable but necessary for survival, organizations can no longer afford the luxury of rigidly defined roles. Instead, the focus has shifted towards cultivating multifaceted professionals who can don the hats of both leader and manager as situations demand.

This is especially true in sectors that are highly volatile and subject to rapid transformation, such as technology, healthcare, and renewable energy. In these industries, professionals must be ready to pivot at a moment's notice. Managers must be able to provide not just logistical but also strategic direction, synthesizing data and insights to inform immediate and long-term planning. They also need to foster an environment where innovation thrives, ensuring that teams have both the resources and the psychological safety to explore new ideas and take calculated risks. In such a setting, managerial tasks extend far beyond administration and into the realms of nurturing creativity and talent development—areas traditionally associated with leadership.

Leaders, for their part, can no longer afford to be aloof visionaries disconnected from the realities of everyday operations. The stakes are too high, and the pace of change too quick, for leaders to operate in a bubble. They need to have a keen understanding of their organizations' operational capabilities, strengths, and weaknesses. Moreover, they must be able to communicate their visions in actionable terms, breaking down grand ideas into implementable steps and milestones. This requires an appreciation for the managerial skills of project planning, performance evaluation, and resource allocation.

The structural changes in organizations also support this convergence. The shift from hierarchical to more flattened organizational models has been facilitated by technological advances. Collaboration tools, project management software, and real-time analytics dashboards are empowering teams to manage themselves more autonomously. Consequently, the role of a central manager or leader directing every action is diminishing. In this environment, responsibilities such as setting the team's direction, motivating colleagues, or resolving conflicts are often shared among team members. This way, everyone gains experience in both managing and leading, further contributing to the merging of these roles.

Even the educational and training programs designed for aspiring managers and leaders are reflecting this convergence. Business schools and corporate training programs are increasingly focusing on a holistic curriculum that encompasses both hard and soft skills. Subjects like emotional intelligence, ethical decision-making, and cultural competency are taught alongside traditional courses in finance, marketing, and operations management. This creates a cadre of professionals who are equally comfortable in strategic planning sessions as they are in operational reviews.

The boundaries between leadership and management are increasingly becoming porous, if not altogether disappearing. The modern professional is expected to be a hybrid, capable of switching between visionary thinking and detail-oriented execution effortlessly. This synthesis of roles is crucial for organizations aiming to stay ahead of the curve in a business landscape characterized by constant flux and uncertainty. It is a transformative evolution, one that promises to make organizations more dynamic, resilient, and ultimately, more successful.

Chapter 2: Core Characteristics of Managers

As we traverse the landscape of modern organizations, the term "management" looms large, a monolith that casts its shadow across every business function and operation. Often enmeshed with leadership yet distinctly unique, management is a construct that is integral to the success, and sometimes the failure, of an organization. But what do we really mean when we talk about management? Is it merely a set of processes designed to ensure organizational efficiency, or does it embody something more profound, a systematic approach to solving complex challenges in a world that is continuously evolving?

In this chapter, we will embark on a journey to unravel the essence of management, delving into its historical underpinnings, exploring its key characteristics, and illuminating the multifaceted role of the modern manager. The objective is not just to define what management is, but to understand why it matters, how its concept has metamorphosed over time, and what it means in the labyrinthine, often unpredictable corridors of today's corporate world.

We begin by tracing the origins and evolution of management as a concept, from its rudimentary forms in ancient civilizations to its current, highly nuanced state. Understanding this evolution is pivotal, for it sets the stage to appreciate the complexities that modern managers face. They are the torchbearers of a legacy that has been shaped by economic shifts, technological advances, and societal changes—a legacy that they must now adapt for the future.

Next, we focus on the key characteristics that form the backbone of management: control, efficiency, and processes. Each of these elements represents a lens through which management can be viewed, a puzzle piece that, when joined with others, creates a comprehensive picture. However, these characteristics are not static; they adapt and morph to fit the needs of different organizational structures and goals.

Finally, we examine the role of the modern manager, a subject of immense scope and variety. Who are these individuals who hold the reins of management, and what exactly is expected of them? We look at the myriad responsibilities that encompass their role, the mindset they employ for problem-solving and optimization, and the unique challenges they face. In understanding these aspects, we also acknowledge the ever-present duality of being a manager: the need to maintain control while encouraging innovation, the challenge of promoting efficiency while not stifling creativity, and the art of establishing processes that are both rigorous and flexible.

As we delve into these themes, our aim is to provide you with a nuanced understanding of management that goes beyond the textbook definitions. We endeavor to present a holistic view, one that respects the rich history of the field while acknowledging the demands of the modern era. So let us embark on this intellectual expedition, armed with curiosity and the eagerness to challenge our preconceived notions about what it truly means to be engaged in the world of management.

Diving into Management: Origins and Evolution

The concept of management has deep historical roots, tracing back to ancient civilizations where the fundamentals of organizing labor and resources were first established. While the term "management" may seem intrinsically tied to the modern era, its principles have been in operation long before the word entered common parlance.

In ancient times, the construction of monumental structures like the pyramids in Egypt or the Great Wall of China required an early form of project management. Though the methods were rudimentary compared to today's standards, they involved elements of planning, resource allocation, and supervision—core tenets of modern management.

However, the term "management" as we understand it today has its roots more closely aligned with the rise of the industrial revolution. The transition from agrarian societies to industrial urban centers necessitated new ways of organizing labor and processes. Theories of management began to develop, culminating in classical approaches like Frederick Taylor's Scientific Management, which emphasized efficiency, standardization, and the optimization of manual labor. Around the same period, Max Weber's theory of bureaucracy laid down the framework for organizational structure, emphasizing hierarchy, defined roles, and a rational-legal authority model. These perspectives set the stage for how management was practiced for a large part of the 20th century—largely mechanistic, heavily process-oriented, and focused on command and control.

However, as business environments became more complex, the limitations of classical management theories became evident. The latter half of the 20th century saw the emergence of more holistic approaches. The Human Relations movement, spearheaded by scholars like Elton Mayo, underscored the importance of social factors in the workplace, including employee morale and group relationships. Management began to be viewed not merely as a set of mechanical tasks but as a complex interplay of relationships, motivations, and human psychology.

In recent decades, the notion of management has evolved yet further to accommodate rapid technological changes, globalization, and the rise of knowledge workers. Today's management theories often focus on adaptability, innovation, and the importance of creating value. Concepts like Lean Management and Agile Methodologies have come to the forefront, prioritizing flexibility, collaboration, and customer focus.

Modern management now encompasses a diverse range of functions, from strategic planning and financial oversight to human resource development and innovation management. In a world characterized by constant change, managers have become orchestrators of adaptability, synthesizing a broad spectrum of tasks and roles. They are expected to be strategic thinkers who can make data-driven decisions, leaders who can inspire teams, and visionaries capable of steering the organization through the tumultuous waters of the modern business landscape.

Management, as a concept and practice, has journeyed from the simple organization of labor to a multifaceted discipline. This evolution reflects the complex, dynamic nature of contemporary organizations and the ever-changing challenges they face.

The arc of management's evolution mirrors the larger currents of human history, sweeping from the simple agricultural societies of yore to today's hyper-connected, technology-driven world. Its progression is not just a linear development, but a reflection of how human endeavors have evolved in complexity, scale, and impact. This journey is best understood as a series of paradigm shifts, each accommodating a new set of challenges and opportunities brought about by technological, social, and economic changes.

From the earliest agrarian societies, management existed as a rudimentary form of organizing labor and resources for survival. But the onset of the industrial revolution in the late 18th and early 19th centuries marked a seismic shift, not just in production methods but in the systematic organization of work. Frederick Taylor's Scientific Management and Max Weber's bureaucratic principles presented a structured, rationalized way of conducting business. It was an era where management was essentially about problem-solving in the most efficient way possible—often at the expense of labor welfare. The emphasis was on functional specializations and hierarchical decision-making, mirroring the machine-like production processes they managed.

As organizations grew in size and complexity, however, the limitations of these early management theories became increasingly evident. This gave rise to the Human Relations movement, which argued that workers are not mere cogs in the machine but social beings whose needs and motivations impact their productivity. Managers began to be seen as not just overseers of work but as facilitators of a conducive work environment, one that recognizes and nurtures the human element. The shift moved the management focus from solely 'task' to a balanced emphasis on 'task and relationship.'

The late 20th and early 21st centuries saw another watershed moment as the digital revolution and globalization converged. This period has been marked by an exponential increase in the volume and velocity of information, requiring management theories to evolve yet again. Today's business landscape requires a kind of managerial agility that was unimaginable in the era of industrial production. Models like Lean and Agile have emerged, focusing on adaptability, iterative learning, and closer customer engagement. Tools such as Business Intelligence, data analytics, and various software systems have become indispensable in decision-making processes.

The term 'manager' is no longer synonymous with top-down authority but implies a multifaceted role. Modern managers are expected to be excellent communicators, empathetic team leaders, skilled negotiators, and strategic planners. They have to navigate cultural, geographic, and disciplinary boundaries as organizations become increasingly diverse and dispersed. As 'knowledge work' has gained prominence, managers have had to become facilitators of creative thinking and innovation, often in flat or matrixed organizational structures where hierarchical authority is less pronounced.

We're also seeing a greater emphasis on ethics and sustainability in management practices. In the face of climate change, social inequality, and heightened scrutiny from stakeholders, contemporary managers are also custodians of corporate social responsibility, often tasked with aligning company goals with broader social and environmental objectives.

In essence, modern management has become a kaleidoscopic discipline, one that changes its patterns and colors in response to the shifting landscape of business, technology, and society. This rich tapestry is what makes the study and practice of management both a challenge and an opportunity, demanding not just a grasp of theories and tools, but also the ability to adapt, empathize, and envision. As we look towards the future, the only constant we can anticipate is change, and it will be the manager's proficiency in navigating this change that will determine organizational success in the days to come.

Key Characteristics of Management

Management, as a field, is rich in variety, complexity, and depth. However, there are certain characteristics that act as its foundational pillars, defining its core essence and setting it apart from other organizational roles like leadership. Let's delve into three key attributes: control, efficiency, and processes.

Control: The Act of Overseeing and Guiding Processes

At the core of any managerial role lies the concept of control. Managers are custodians of organizational resources, be they human, financial, or material. This custodianship extends to processes, tasks, and even intangibles like organizational culture. Control does not imply micromanagement or the suppression of creativity. Rather, it denotes the ability to steer these resources effectively toward the achievement of specific goals.

The act of control involves monitoring performance, making timely interventions to correct course, and ensuring that every part of the system is aligned with the broader objectives. Control also requires a keen understanding of each team member's capabilities and challenges so that resources can be allocated, and tasks delegated in a way that maximizes collective performance.

Control in management extends far beyond merely overseeing day-to-day operations. It involves a complex layering of roles that intersects with other managerial functions like planning, organizing, and leading. Managers employ various types of control: feedforward control to proactively shape the conditions leading to outcomes, concurrent control to manage processes as they occur, and feedback control to assess performance and make necessary adjustments. Each type plays a role in ensuring that the organization stays aligned with its strategic objectives.

Traditionally, control was implemented through a top-down hierarchy, where senior managers set the goals, and lower-level managers executed them. However, with the advent of agile and decentralized organizational structures, control mechanisms have become more collaborative and adaptive. This shift has led to a more nuanced understanding of control, which can be both empowering and participative, rather than restrictive.

Effective control is also closely tied to measurement. Performance metrics, key performance indicators (KPIs), and balanced scorecards are some of the tools used to quantify performance. These metrics are essential for establishing a baseline, setting goals, and tracking progress. They also provide an empirical foundation for decision-making, allowing managers to identify bottlenecks, allocate resources more effectively, and anticipate future challenges.

But control is not just a mechanistic function. It also involves an emotional and psychological dimension. A good manager understands the importance of maintaining morale, fostering a positive work environment, and inspiring the team. For instance, control over the organizational culture is a soft, often underemphasized aspect of managerial control, but it significantly impacts productivity, employee satisfaction, and, ultimately, organizational success. A strong culture can act as a self-regulating mechanism, encouraging employees to take ownership of their tasks and align themselves with organizational objectives.

Moreover, the act of control extends to crisis management and risk mitigation. Contingency planning, scenario analyses, and proactive identification of risks are an integral part of a manager's control function. These aspects have gained prominence in an era characterized by uncertainty and volatility. The COVID-19 pandemic is a case in point, underscoring the need for agile control mechanisms that can adapt to rapidly changing circumstances.

Control in the modern sense is, therefore, a balancing act. On the one hand, it requires rigor, discipline, and an analytical approach to monitoring and intervention. On the other, it demands emotional intelligence, adaptability, and an understanding of human dynamics. In a world where organizations are increasingly complex, networked, and subject to rapid change, the act of control has evolved from a one-dimensional task of oversight to a multi-dimensional skill that intersects with virtually every aspect of management. Effective control is thus less about imposing rigid structures and more about creating an environment where both the organization and its members can achieve their fullest potential.

Efficiency: Maximizing Outputs While Minimizing Inputs

Another defining characteristic of management is the emphasis on efficiency. The ideal manager is adept at getting the most out of limited resources. This goes beyond mere cost-cutting or speed; it involves the optimization of workflows, the elimination of bottlenecks, and the continuous improvement of processes to achieve higher productivity.

Efficiency is intertwined with metrics, and any discussion on it invariably leads to the tools and techniques that managers use to measure performance. Key Performance Indicators (KPIs), Return on Investment (ROI), and other metrics often serve as the compass that guides managerial decisions. By optimizing for efficiency, managers help create value for stakeholders ranging from employees and customers to shareholders.

The concept of efficiency has been integral to management since its early formulations in the industrial era. Figures like Frederick Taylor, known as the father of Scientific Management, put a heavy emphasis on the systematic study of work methods to improve efficiency. However, the understanding and application of efficiency have evolved considerably to adapt to today's increasingly complex and dynamic business environment.

Modern approaches to efficiency take a more holistic view, recognizing that maximizing outputs and minimizing inputs requires a multi-faceted strategy. It's not just about increasing the speed of production but about improving the quality of outputs, reducing waste, and enhancing the overall effectiveness of the organization. Terms like "lean management," which originated in manufacturing but have broad applications, encapsulate this nuanced understanding. Lean principles focus on creating more value with fewer resources by optimizing the flow of products and services through entire value streams that flow horizontally across technologies, assets, and departments to customers.

Technological advances, particularly in data analytics and automation, have further nuanced our understanding of efficiency. Data analytics tools allow managers to monitor various metrics in real-time, providing insights that were previously impossible or very time-consuming to obtain. Machine learning algorithms can predict bottlenecks and inefficiencies, enabling proactive interventions. Automation and Artificial Intelligence (AI) are increasingly being used to handle repetitive tasks, freeing human resources to focus on more complex, value-added activities.

It isn't solely a matter of numbers and technology. It also involves human elements like employee satisfaction, skills development, and workplace culture. An efficient organization is one where employees are engaged, well-trained, and aligned with the company's goals. Studies have shown that engaged employees are more productive, which in turn enhances overall efficiency. Therefore, modern managers view efficiency not just through a financial lens but also through a human one. Techniques like job enrichment, flexible work arrangements, and team-building exercises are now considered integral to building an efficient organization.

Efficiency also extends to sustainable practices, which have become increasingly important in today's world. Concepts like "sustainable efficiency" or "triple bottom line" (considering social and environmental performance alongside financial performance) have emerged, pushing managers to think long-term and consider the broader impact of their decisions.

In summary, efficiency in modern management is a multi-dimensional construct. It is as much about optimizing workflows and leveraging technology as it is about nurturing human potential and adopting sustainable practices. Achieving efficiency requires a blend of analytical rigor, technological savvy, and a deep understanding of human psychology and organizational culture. In a world of finite resources but infinite possibilities, efficiency remains a cornerstone of effective management.

Processes: Establishing and Refining Systems for Consistency

The final cornerstone we examine is that of processes. Processes can be considered the architecture within which control and efficiency operate. They provide the structural integrity that enables an organization to function smoothly, offering a standardized way of executing tasks, solving problems, and delivering results.

Processes are the frameworks that guide action, provide accountability, and yield reproducible results. Well-designed processes allow for innovation within defined parameters, creating an environment where creativity and control coexist. Managers are often responsible for either establishing these processes from the ground up or refining existing systems to adapt to changing needs and circumstances.

The establishment and refinement of processes are critical tasks that require a thorough understanding of the organization's objectives, the specific requirements of various functions, and the interactions among different departments. In essence, a well-laid-out process serves as a roadmap for execution, clarifying roles, responsibilities, and workflows. Processes act as safeguards, ensuring that tasks are executed correctly and that everyone in the organization is aligned toward common goals.

In the early phases of an organization or project, processes might be loose, flexible, and adaptive, largely because the focus is usually on quick market entry, innovation, or problem-solving. However, as organizations scale, the need for structured processes becomes increasingly evident. Lack of standardized processes can lead to inefficiency, errors, and even organizational dysfunction. Therefore, one of the key roles of a manager is to recognize when an organization has reached a point where process formalization becomes imperative.

There's a delicate balance to be struck between over-engineering and under-engineering processes. Too much rigidity can stifle creativity and adaptability. Too little can result in chaos, inconsistency, and unreliability. Striking the right balance often involves a cycle of design, implementation, monitoring, and refinement. Continuous process improvement methodologies, such as Six Sigma or Total Quality Management (TQM), are geared toward this, focusing on ongoing improvement to drive an organization's output quality towards perfection.

Processes are not static; they need to evolve with the business landscape. Market conditions, customer needs, and technological advancements all require processes to be agile and adaptable. For instance, the advent of digital transformation initiatives in many organizations has necessitated rethinking traditional processes to integrate digital technologies, enabling quicker decisions, better customer engagement, and more efficient operations.

The role of technology in process management cannot be overstated. Tools like Business Process Management (BPM) software and workflow automation platforms have revolutionized how processes are mapped, executed, and monitored. They offer real-time insights into performance, thereby allowing managers to make data-driven decisions to tweak processes for optimal results.

Processes also play a crucial role in risk management. Standardized procedures provide a blueprint for decision-making under various scenarios, often including contingencies for unexpected situations. This aids in making the organization more resilient and better prepared to navigate the challenges that come its way.

Processes serve as the operational backbone of an organization. They provide the structure and guidelines within which an organization's myriad activities take place. By meticulously designing and continually refining these processes, managers contribute to building organizations that are not only efficient and controlled but also adaptable and resilient. Given the rapid pace of change in today's business environment, the ability to master process management is more critical than ever for modern managers.

In summary, control, efficiency, and processes are interrelated facets that together encapsulate the essence of management. These characteristics do not operate in isolation but interact in complex ways to define the role of a manager. They form the substratum upon which other managerial skills and strategies are built, offering a sturdy platform for achieving organizational objectives. As we proceed through this book, these foundational elements will recur, underlining their enduring relevance in the ever-evolving field of management.

The Role of a Manager

Having established the foundational elements that characterize management, it's important to delve into the practical aspects—the daily life and challenges that define the role of a modern manager. Here, we explore their day-to-day responsibilities, the mindset that fuels their actions, and the hurdles they inevitably encounter.

The Day-to-Day Responsibilities

The managerial role is a tapestry woven from threads of diverse responsibilities that require continuous attention, adaptation, and skill. Far from being a monolithic or static set of tasks, the daily agenda of a manager can be likened to a dynamic ecosystem, where responsibilities across various domains interact and influence each other in intricate ways.

Human Resources Management

On any given day, a manager may find themselves at the epicenter of human resource-related activities. This could involve interviewing potential candidates, conducting performance reviews, or managing team dynamics to ensure a healthy and productive work environment. It may also involve conflict resolution—addressing issues between team members or departments to ensure seamless collaboration and productivity. Thus, people management becomes a cornerstone of a manager's daily responsibilities.

Project Oversight

Alongside human resources, project management often occupies a large slice of a manager's time. Ensuring that all projects are on track, identifying bottlenecks, and allocating resources effectively are part of this domain. If a project is falling behind, it's the manager's duty to identify the reasons and implement changes to get things back on track. The challenge here is often balancing quality with speed, and short-term gains with long-term objectives.

Strategic Planning

Although this might not be a daily task, strategic planning is a frequent component of a manager's schedule. This involves liaising with upper management and other stakeholders to align the department's activities with the organization's overarching goals. It could be about launching a new product, entering a new market, or pivoting the business model. The manager has to consider the immediate needs of the team alongside the longer-term implications for the organization.

Financial Management

Budgeting, forecasting, and financial planning are not just the realm of CFOs. Managers often have budgetary responsibilities that impact their teams and projects directly. This means keeping an eye on expenditures, ensuring they align with budget constraints, and optimizing for cost-efficiency. Whether they are approving purchase orders or negotiating with vendors, financial acumen is a must-have skill in their toolkit.

Communication and Stakeholder Management

No manager is an island. A considerable amount of their time is spent communicating—be it through team meetings, one-on-one sessions, or emails. They also interface with various stakeholders, including senior management, other departments, and external partners like clients and vendors. Communication skills become pivotal, as miscommunication can lead to misunderstandings, delays, or even project failures.

Problem-Solving On-the-Fly

Amidst all these planned and structured activities, unexpected challenges inevitably arise. A vendor may miss a deadline, a key team member could fall sick, or a sudden market shift may necessitate a change in strategy. A manager's day is rarely predictable, and they need to be prepared to handle immediate issues that threaten to derail ongoing projects or team dynamics.

The daily life of a manager is a kaleidoscope of multifaceted tasks that require them to switch roles frequently—from being a strategist one moment to a problem-solver the next. It's this variety and unpredictability that make the role of a manager both exciting and demanding, requiring a blend of skills that are as diverse as the tasks they undertake.

The Mindset of Problem-Solving and Optimization

Inhabiting the role of a manager requires a certain mindset—one that thrives on problem-solving and optimization. Managers are the go-to people when there are challenges that require immediate resolution. Whether it's a performance issue with a team member or a glitch in a project's timeline, managers are expected to arrive at solutions that are both effective and efficient.

The skill to optimize comes into play here. Given that resources are always finite, managers must make decisions that maximize outcomes while minimizing costs, whether it's in terms of time, manpower, or capital. This requires a unique blend of analytical thinking, creativity, and pragmatism. Managers often have to 'think on their feet,' adapting to the fluidity and unpredictability that characterize most modern workplaces.

The mindset of problem-solving often starts with a diagnostic approach. Managers must first accurately identify the issue at hand, dissecting it into its constituent elements to better understand its scope, impact, and underlying causes. This involves both qualitative and quantitative analysis, employing tools like SWOT (Strengths, Weaknesses, Opportunities, and Threats) analyses, root cause identification, or even more advanced statistical methods like regression analysis for complex problems.

Once the problem is adequately diagnosed, the optimization process begins. This is where the ability to critically evaluate different courses of action comes into play. Managers must weigh the pros and cons of various solutions, taking into consideration a myriad of factors such as short-term gains, long-term sustainability, resource availability, and alignment with organizational goals. In essence, the optimization phase is a balancing act that seeks to achieve the most favorable outcome under given constraints.

The problem-solving and optimization mindset also necessitates a proclivity for continuous improvement. In a rapidly changing business environment, what worked yesterday might not necessarily be the best solution for today. Managers, therefore, must adopt a cyclical approach to problem-solving, one that incorporates regular feedback and iterative adjustments.

Approaches like the Plan-Do-Check-Act (PDCA) cycle or Agile methodologies advocate for this sort of ongoing optimization.

Creativity is another key aspect of this mindset. While analytical skills are invaluable for diagnosing problems and evaluating solutions, creativity is what enables managers to conceive of those solutions in the first place. Whether it's finding a novel way to streamline a process, or brainstorming a unique solution to a customer issue, creative thinking expands the range of possible solutions, increasing the odds of arriving at an optimal outcome.

It's also essential to highlight the role of emotional intelligence in this mindset. The best problem-solvers are not just analytically adept; they are also skilled at managing emotions, both their own and those of their team. Problem-solving is often a high-pressure endeavor, fraught with uncertainty and potentially charged with emotional volatility. Being able to maintain composure, inspire confidence, and manage stress are crucial traits that can significantly impact the quality of decision-making.

Moreover, managers need to be adept at change management as problem-solving often involves altering existing processes, roles, or even entire business models. Being able to guide a team through the turbulent waters of change, addressing concerns, and ensuring smooth transitions is an invaluable skill.

The Challenges Faced and How They're Typically Addressed

The complexities of the managerial role extend far beyond the daily grind of tasks and responsibilities; they penetrate into the arena of challenges that managers inevitably face. In the intricate fabric of modern business operations, interpersonal conflicts within the team can arise, simmering beneath the surface and sometimes erupting into open discord. These conflicts can be as minor as a disagreement over a project approach or as major as clashing work styles that disrupt team cohesion. Regardless of scale, it's the manager's responsibility to mediate, bringing resolution that sustains both productivity and workplace harmony.

Navigating the maze of organizational politics is another area of challenge. Every organization has its culture, power structures, and unwritten rules. Managers are often at the crossroads of these dynamics, having to delicately balance the interests and influences from above and below, all while maintaining their professional integrity. It's not uncommon for them to be the intermediary between the executive team and frontline employees, carrying messages and mandates in both directions.

External pressures add another layer to the challenges managers face. Market competition is perpetually evolving, often requiring rapid adjustments to strategies and execution. In highly regulated industries, legislative changes can suddenly come into play, necessitating quick, sweeping modifications to processes or even business models. Customer expectations also never remain static; the constant evolution of technology and social trends means that what satisfied customers yesterday might not tomorrow. Managers need to keep their fingers on the pulse of these external factors, ensuring that their teams adapt and evolve accordingly.

Confronting these challenges is seldom straightforward and rarely involves a one-size-fits-all solution. Managers find themselves having to employ a multifaceted approach, pulling from a diverse skill set that includes negotiation capabilities, strategic foresight, and crisis management skills. For instance, resolving interpersonal conflicts may require negotiation skills to reach a compromise acceptable to all parties involved. Strategic planning becomes essential when adapting to market competition or regulatory changes, allowing the manager to map out new routes to success while mitigating risks. Crisis management comes to the fore when unexpected events threaten to derail projects or tarnish the team's performance.

But even skills and strategies can only go so far without the right relational dynamics. Effective management of challenges often necessitates collaboration. Managers frequently have to reach out to other team members, consult with peer managers, and engage stakeholders in dialogue to come to viable solutions. The ability to work together as part of a larger organism underlines the importance of a manager's social skills, which can often make or break their success in overcoming challenges.

The role of feedback—both giving and receiving—cannot be overstated. A manager's openness to feedback can serve as an invaluable tool for personal and professional growth. Whether the feedback comes from higher-ups assessing project outcomes, or from team members sharing their workplace experience, it offers an opportunity for learning. The ability to not only hear but also to integrate this feedback is vital for managerial development. It complements another critical trait: the ability to learn from both successes and failures. Each challenge provides a lesson and each solution, whether successful or not, provides a blueprint for future challenges.

It is clear that the role of a manager is a complex tapestry of challenges that extend across the personal, organizational, and even market-wide scales. And meeting these challenges requires an equally complex range of strategies, skills, and sensitivities. It is this demanding yet rewarding confluence of requirements that marks the essence of modern managerial roles, requiring a lifelong commitment to learning, adaptation, and interpersonal engagement.

As we conclude this chapter, it's worth reflecting on the journey we've undertaken to dissect and analyze the evolving roles of leadership and management. We have moved from the assembly lines of Henry Ford to the agile and interconnected workplaces of the 21st century, tracing the transformation of what it means to lead and manage in contemporary organizations. This complex tapestry of changes reflects the broader shifts in society, technology, and the global economy—making the topics of management and leadership more dynamic and pertinent than ever before.

We have explored how efficiency and standardization, the watchwords of yesteryears, have been complemented by ingenuity, adaptability, and emotional intelligence. We delved into the pivotal transitions—how managers today are expected to be more than process custodians, and how leaders are required to be astutely aware of the operational realities of their visions. Most importantly, we examined the convergence of these roles, emphasizing the importance of hybrid skill sets that serve the multidimensional demands of modern organizations.

Our intent has been to offer you more than just an academic overview. The aim is to equip you with a multifaceted understanding, one that enables you to critically evaluate scenarios, adapt to new challenges, and excel in whichever capacity you serve—be it as a manager, a leader, or the increasingly common hybrid of both. We hope that this chapter has not only broadened your conceptual horizons but also triggered introspection about your own role and potential.

As we transition to the subsequent chapters, where real-world case studies and future trends in leadership and management will be discussed, it is this foundational understanding that will add depth to our explorations. While the landscape of leadership and management will continue to evolve, the core principles rooted in human collaboration, ethical conduct, and shared purpose remain unchanging. These principles act as our guiding stars as we navigate the fluctuating seas of professional life.

Chapter 3: Core Characteristics of Leaders

The discourse around leadership has long fascinated scholars, practitioners, and observers alike. The subject is as ancient as human civilization itself, imbued with myths, stories, and archetypes that have not only guided empires and revolutions but also fueled innovation and progress in every field imaginable. Yet despite the historical gravitas and the voluminous studies devoted to it, leadership remains an enigma — a complex interplay of traits, skills, and situational factors that defy easy explanation or categorization.

In this chapter, we delve into the multi-faceted world of leadership. We begin by tracing back its origins and historical transformations, exploring how it has evolved from the time of kings and warriors to today's inclusive, participatory paradigms. Then we examine its key characteristics, including the ability to inspire and motivate, the clarity of vision, and the courage to challenge the status quo. These are the elements that distinguish leaders from mere managers and position them as transformative figures capable of changing not just businesses but societies at large.

We'll also delve into the role a leader plays in today's complex, fast-paced organizational landscape. Here, we go beyond the spotlight that shines on the individual to examine how a leader sets the course for teams and organizations, fosters a positive culture, and navigates the inevitable challenges and uncertainties that come with pushing boundaries and seeking innovation.

As we journey through this chapter, you will find that leadership is not just a set of isolated qualities that one possesses but a dynamic process that one engages in. It's a craft that requires lifelong learning, an openness to change, and above all, a deep-rooted commitment to bring out the best in oneself and others.

Origins and Evolution: The Transformative Journey of Leadership

The concept of leadership is as old as human history, appearing in the annals of virtually every culture and civilization. From tribal chieftains and ancient kings to modern-day presidents and CEOs, the essence of leadership has been shaped by various factors, including societal values, technological advancements, and historical events.

In its earliest form, leadership was often closely tied to physical prowess and the ability to protect the community. The leader was typically the strongest, bravest member of the tribe, responsible for making decisions that would ensure the group's survival. As societies became more complex, transitioning from hunter-gatherer communities to agricultural settlements and eventually into organized states and empires, the role of the leader evolved as well. Physical might gave way to strategic intelligence, and the act of governing became increasingly intricate, necessitating specialized skills in diplomacy, law, and administration.

With the advent of the Renaissance and the Enlightenment, ideas about leadership began to shift yet again. Philosophers and scholars introduced concepts such as the social contract and the separation of powers, reshaping the perception of leadership from a divine right to a negotiated relationship between the leader and the led. The implications were profound: leadership was no longer seen as a static position, but rather a dynamic role that required the consent and collaboration of those being led.

The 20th century brought about another significant evolution in leadership, influenced by both world wars, the civil rights movements, globalization, and the digital revolution. The notion of leadership became democratized, opening up the field to individuals regardless of their social standing, ethnicity, or gender. Technological advancements and the rise of knowledge economies put a premium on intellectual capital, leading to the increasing importance of visionary, inspirational leadership. No longer was it sufficient for a leader to simply manage resources and oversee operations. They were expected to be innovators, change-makers, and influencers.

And now, as we navigate the complexities of the 21st century—a world that is increasingly interconnected, volatile, and diverse—the role of leadership continues to adapt. Modern leadership is characterized by terms such as 'servant leadership,' 'transformational leadership,' and 'authentic leadership,' reflecting an even greater emphasis on empathy, ethics, and emotional intelligence. Leaders today are expected to be both globally minded and locally responsible, able to leverage technology and yet sensitive to the human needs of their followers.

The transformation of leadership over time has been both significant and, in many ways, cyclical. While the core functions of providing direction, offering protection, and solving problems have remained, the ways these functions are fulfilled have evolved dramatically. We've moved from brute strength to strategic acumen, from autocratic rule to collaborative governance, and from operational oversight to inspirational vision.

As we continue to face new challenges and opportunities, the concept of leadership will undoubtedly continue to evolve. But understanding its origins and the various transformations it has undergone over millennia is crucial for anyone aspiring to be an effective leader in today's complex world. This historical lens offers not just perspective but also inspiration, reminding us that at its core, leadership has always been about enabling a group of people to achieve a common goal. And how we do that is the ever-unfolding story of leadership.

Key Characteristics of Leadership: The Building Blocks of Influence and Impact

While leadership has taken on various forms and meanings over the course of history, there are fundamental characteristics that remain central to the concept. These characteristics not only distinguish leaders from others but also serve as the pillars upon which effective leadership is built. Here we delve into three such key traits: the ability to inspire, the clarity of vision, and the courage to challenge the status quo.

Inspiration: The Ability to Ignite Passion and Motivation

Inspiration is the spark that sets the fire of achievement alight. Leaders inspire by tapping into the hopes, aspirations, and potential of those around them. They don't just set targets; they make people want to reach for the stars. Whether it's through compelling storytelling, emotional intelligence, or the sheer force of a charismatic personality, inspiring leaders create an emotional connection that motivates individuals to go above and beyond what they initially thought possible. Importantly, this inspirational power isn't about dictating action, but rather fostering an environment where people feel empowered to act themselves.

In an organizational setting, the ability to inspire is an indispensable asset, going hand-in-hand with the hard skills of project management, strategy development, and operational oversight. Inspiration is the catalyst that transforms a well-crafted plan into a passionately executed mission, transforming the mundane into the magical and the improbable into the achievable.

Several key components underlie the ability to inspire effectively:

☐ Authenticity: Authentic leaders inspire trust and devotion because they are true to themselves and transparent with others. This authenticity fosters deeper relationships, which in turn creates a stronger emotional connection, making it easier to inspire those they lead.

☐ Empathy: Understanding the individual needs, aspirations, and challenges of team members allows a leader to connect in a more personal and effective manner. Empathy enables targeted inspiration, tailored to the specific circumstances and requirements of each individual.

☐ Resilience and Optimism: Challenges and setbacks are inevitable, but inspiring leaders maintain a positive outlook even in the face of adversity. Their resilience acts as a beacon, guiding team members through difficulties and instilling in them the confidence that obstacles can be overcome.

☐ Leading by Example: Perhaps one of the most potent ways to inspire is to lead by example. When leaders embody the values, work ethic, and commitment they preach, it serves as a powerful motivator for their team to do the same.

☐ Communication Skills: Effective storytelling, persuasive rhetoric, and clear, open dialogue are all important tools in the inspiring leader's arsenal. These skills allow leaders to frame challenges and opportunities in ways that stir emotion and incite action.

☐ Encouragement and Recognition: Acknowledging and celebrating achievements, no matter how small, can have a profound impact on morale and motivation. This form of positive reinforcement not only boosts individual ego but also strengthens team cohesion.

☐ Empowerment: Inspiring leaders don't hoard power; they distribute it. They offer team members opportunities to take on responsibilities, make decisions, and contribute their ideas. This empowerment fosters a sense of ownership and investment among team members, further enhancing their motivation to achieve collective goals.

☐ Learning and Development: Inspiration often comes from growth and development. By encouraging and facilitating continuous learning, leaders signal their investment in the personal and professional growth of their team, making them more eager to reciprocate with dedication and hard work.

In essence, the ability to inspire transcends the transactional dimensions of the workplace to engage with the emotional and psychological core of each team member. It melds together the objective and the subjective, creating a synergistic effect that propels organizations toward unparalleled achievement. Inspiring leaders cultivate a culture where passion and purpose are not just buzzwords but are the very fabric that holds the organization together. They turn the aspirational into the operational and make the incredible feel inevitable.

Vision: Seeing the Bigger Picture and Setting a Direction

The best leaders are also visionaries. They have the ability to see beyond the immediate, to discern underlying patterns, and to look at the world not just as it is but as it could be. This vision acts as a North Star, providing direction and purpose not only for the leader but also for the team or organization they guide. By painting a compelling picture of the future, a visionary leader helps to align the energies and focus of various stakeholders towards shared goals. Moreover, having a clear vision can be particularly crucial in times of uncertainty or crisis, offering a stable point of orientation when the path ahead seems unclear.

The act of envisioning the future transcends mere goal setting; it involves creating a vivid mental landscape that encapsulates the ethos, ambitions, and potential transformations that could redefine an organization's path. It's not just about milestones and key performance indicators, although those are important. Vision is more ethereal, blending rationality with imagination, facts with aspirations, and present realities with future possibilities.

Having a well-articulated vision serves as a unifying force, aligning different departments, functions, and even external partners around a common purpose. The vision becomes a storytelling tool, a narrative that makes complex strategies relatable and abstract missions palpable. It weaves together the various threads of an organization's activities into a cohesive tapestry that everyone can understand and contribute to.

In a world where distractions are numerous and the competition for mental bandwidth is intense, a compelling vision helps to maintain focus and consistency across actions and decisions. It acts as a sieve, helping to prioritize resources and efforts by aligning them with the broader objectives. This sort of alignment is essential for any organization, but it is especially vital in larger or more complex entities where the risks of fragmentation and internal conflict are greater.

Notably, a vision isn't a fixed point but a guiding star. It allows for course corrections, adapts to new information, and evolves as circumstances dictate, yet it remains a source of inspiration and guidance. By being both steadfast and flexible, the vision provides room for innovation, encouraging team members to explore, challenge, and refine the organization's strategic direction.

A leader's vision is also their most potent tool for inspiring people. A compelling vision evokes emotion—it excites, intrigues, and motivates. It makes the challenges seem worth tackling and turns work into a quest for something greater. Importantly, vision also provides a sense of safety and confidence in uncertain times. It is a lighthouse in the fog of uncertainty, its constant glow a reassurance that there's a direction, a plan, and a future worth striving for.

A vision offers more than a map for the future; it offers a sense of identity. It tells team members and stakeholders who they are, who they can become, and how they fit into the larger story. Thus, the role of a visionary leader is not just to set targets but to provide a framework within which individuals find meaning, purpose, and a sense of belonging. Through vision, a leader transforms a group of individuals into a focused, collaborative, and purpose-driven team.

Challenging the Status Quo: The Courage to Seek Change and Innovation

Leadership often involves breaking out of established norms to pursue something greater. This requires courage—another integral trait of effective leaders. It's not just about taking risks but also about challenging existing systems, questioning conventional wisdom, and being willing to innovate. A leader's courage manifests in their ability to push boundaries, disrupt complacent practices, and introduce new paradigms. This might mean advocating for an unpopular yet necessary change, pioneering a groundbreaking product, or taking a moral stand. The courage to challenge the status quo is often what separates leaders who leave a lasting impact from those who merely occupy a position of authority.

The essence of challenging the status quo lies in a leader's ability to cultivate a culture of constructive dissent, intellectual curiosity, and continuous improvement. Such leaders create environments where questioning is encouraged and where the prevailing wisdom is not taken as gospel but as a hypothesis open to scrutiny. This environment is not confrontational but is designed to elevate an organization through collective, collaborative effort. By refusing to settle for "good enough," such leaders communicate an unspoken ethos—that there is always room for growth, for questioning, for striving towards excellence.

Leaders with the courage to challenge existing norms also recognize the importance of timing. They understand that not every moment is ripe for disruption or transformation. As much as they are inclined towards action, they also know when to exercise restraint, to observe, to listen, and to wait for the opportune moment when their call for change will have the maximum resonance and the greatest chance of success. They weigh the risks and rewards, aware that the sustainability of change relies on its timing, its context, and its relevance to those who are expected to adapt.

Challenging the status quo doesn't mean change for change's sake. It is purpose-driven, grounded in a leader's overarching vision and aligned with the organization's long-term strategic goals. Every step taken, every norm questioned, and every boundary pushed is done with a clear understanding of how such actions serve to further that vision. This targeted focus ensures that change is constructive, not destructive; it evolves the organization rather than creating chaos.

Leaders who have the courage to challenge the status quo understand that they can't—and shouldn't—do it alone. They rally their teams, solicit input, and build coalitions. They recognize that the most impactful changes often come from the bottom up, from the team members who are closest to the work, the customers, or the challenges at hand. By involving a diverse range of perspectives, leaders not only build buy-in but also enrich their own understanding, enhancing the quality of the change they seek to implement.

In the grand scheme of things, a leader's willingness to challenge the status quo contributes to their legacy. It defines how they are remembered and the impact they leave behind. Those who are courageous enough to seek change and innovation not only elevate themselves but lift the entire organization to new heights. They set the stage for ongoing growth, resilience, and adaptability, anchoring the organization in a culture that views change not as a threat but as an opportunity for continual renewal and advancement.

These key characteristics—inspiration, vision, and courage—serve as the bedrock of leadership. They are the elements that energize teams, shape cultures, and drive change. While the way these characteristics manifest can differ from one leader to another, their essence remains the same: to mobilize individuals towards a shared purpose, and in doing so, achieve something extraordinary. As we move forward into an era that demands both adaptability and integrity, these foundational traits are more important than ever for anyone aspiring to lead effectively.

The Role of a Leader: Charting the Course, Shaping the Culture, and Weathering the Storm

Leadership is not an abstract concept but a tangible role with specific responsibilities that have far-reaching implications. In modern organizations, a leader's job is complex and multi-dimensional. Let's consider the different facets that comprise the role of a leader in today's world.

Setting the Vision and Direction for Teams or Entire Organizations

One of the primary responsibilities of a leader is to set the vision and direction for the team or organization they lead. This vision serves as a strategic roadmap, outlining where the group is headed and how it aims to get there. The leader articulates this vision in a way that is compelling and relatable, thereby inspiring team members to engage with the mission passionately. More than just a statement, the vision becomes the ideological backbone of the organization, influencing decision-making at every level. The leader is responsible for ensuring that this vision is not only communicated but also integrated into the organization's culture and operations.

Building and Fostering a Positive Organizational Culture

Culture is often described as "the way things are done around here," and leaders play a pivotal role in establishing and nurturing it. A positive organizational culture can serve as a competitive advantage, helping to attract talent, foster innovation, and build a cohesive team. Leaders build culture not just through policies and incentives but also through their own behavior, which sets the tone for the entire organization. They recognize the value of diversity, promote a sense of belonging, and create an environment where open dialogue and collaboration flourish. By doing so, they lay the foundation for a culture that is adaptable, resilient, and poised for long-term success.

Navigating Through Challenges and Uncertainties with Resilience

The journey towards achieving a vision is seldom smooth. Along the way, leaders must navigate a range of challenges and uncertainties that can range from market fluctuations and competitive pressures to internal conflicts and resource constraints. How a leader handles these challenges often sets the tone for the entire organization. Resilience, in this context, is not just about bouncing back from setbacks but also about anticipating potential obstacles and preparing for them. Leaders demonstrate resilience by maintaining a positive outlook, adapting to change, and encouraging their teams to do the same. They don't just solve problems; they turn challenges into opportunities for growth and learning.

In a world that seems increasingly volatile, uncertain, complex, and ambiguous, the role of a leader extends far beyond the transactional elements of management. The leader is the linchpin, the visionary, and the moral compass, guiding an organization through the labyrinthine challenges of modern business. While technical skills and expertise remain important, it is the softer skills—empathy, courage, and the ability to inspire—that often distinguish great leaders from merely competent ones.

The convergence of management and leadership roles in the modern workspace also points to a nuanced understanding that leadership is not confined to a designated position or title. It is a behavior, an attitude, a way of approaching challenges and opportunities that can manifest at any level within an organization. Leaders exist in every department, at every level, and their influence is often magnified when they operate synergistically, guided by a unified vision.

This evolving landscape of leadership demands adaptability, a deep sense of self-awareness, and an enduring commitment to personal and professional growth. The most effective leaders will be those who continuously strive to better themselves, who are unafraid to question their own assumptions, and who view leadership not as a goal to be achieved but as a journey of constant learning and self-discovery.

In the final analysis, the measure of a leader's worth is in the value they add to others, in the cultures they cultivate, and in the visions, they help to make a reality. As we move forward in this age of relentless change, the leader's compass must be set by values that endure—the principles of integrity, respect, and a shared sense of purpose that can weather any storm.

As we conclude this exploration of leadership in modern times, let's remember that leadership is not just an individual pursuit but a collective endeavor. It requires the leader to be deeply attuned to the needs, aspirations, and potential of those they lead, to inspire them toward common goals, and to facilitate an environment where every team member feels empowered to contribute their unique skills and perspectives.

The art of leadership, therefore, is in balancing the complexities and contradictions that come with this important role: being visionary yet grounded, strategic yet responsive, confident yet humble. By understanding and integrating these multi-dimensional aspects of leadership, future leaders will be better prepared to navigate the intricacies of contemporary organizations, driving not only their personal success but the enduring prosperity of the communities they serve.

Chapter 4: The Overlaps: Where Management Meets Leadership

In the preceding chapters, we've dissected the complex realms of management and leadership, illuminating their unique traits, origins, and evolutions. While it's beneficial to understand these roles in isolation, the reality of modern organizational life tells a different story—one where the lines between management and leadership frequently blur. This duality is not an aberration but rather a necessity. Today's fast-paced, highly competitive, and increasingly complex business environment requires professionals who can not only manage tasks but also lead people, who can not only maintain systems but also inspire change.

This chapter aims to delve into the interplay between management and leadership. We'll explore this intricate relationship through a kaleidoscope of angles—from the areas where the two overlap to the roles that necessitate a blend of both skill sets. We will move beyond theoretical paradigms to examine real-world implications, providing concrete examples and case studies to drive home the point.

Why is this important? For one, understanding this overlap can free you from the limitations of labels. No longer do you need to box yourself into the category of "manager" or "leader" when the reality is that you are likely both, to varying degrees and in different circumstances. Second, recognizing the symbiosis between management and leadership can offer a competitive advantage. It equips professionals and organizations with a broader set of tools to navigate the challenges and opportunities that lie ahead.

So, as we delve into this complex intersection of disciplines, let us keep in mind that our ultimate aim is not merely to define or differentiate but to integrate and harmonize. In an age where adaptability is key, embracing the overlaps between leadership and management could very well be the linchpin of organizational excellence and personal career success.

The Grey Area: Where Management and Leadership Overlap

It's tempting to imagine a clearly defined boundary between management and leadership—two distinct circles with no points of intersection. The real world, however, is much more akin to a Venn diagram, with a significant overlapping space where the two circles meet. Within this "grey area," roles and responsibilities often demand a seamless integration of both management and leadership competencies. Let's delve into this critical zone to unpack its complexities.

Common Functions and Responsibilities

Several core functions within an organization call for a blend of management and leadership skills. Strategic planning, for example, requires the vision to chart a forward-looking course (leadership) and the meticulous attention to detail needed to craft a roadmap for achieving that vision (management). Similarly, crisis management often calls for rapid decision-making and a strong guiding hand to navigate the team through choppy waters (leadership), coupled with effective resource allocation and a contingency plan (management).

Another common function is team development. Here, the managerial skill of performance assessment dovetails with the leadership ability to inspire and mentor. After all, team members look up to a figure who can not only point out their areas for improvement but also guide them on a transformative journey toward betterment.

Human resource management is yet another arena where management and leadership overlap. While the administrative tasks of recruitment, payroll, and policy enforcement fall under traditional managerial roles, the leadership aspects come into play in areas like organizational culture building, employee engagement, and talent development. Managers who are also leaders are more likely to retain top talent because they invest in the growth and well-being of their staff. They know when to wear the "manager's hat," focusing on procedures and outcomes, and when to switch to the "leader's hat," inspiring trust and fostering a sense of purpose.

Financial management is another dual responsibility. While the manager ensures budget adherence, optimal resource allocation, and fiscal reporting, the leader in the same role looks at financial metrics as tools for strategic decision-making. This involves making investments for long-term gains or choosing a financial path that aligns with the company's ethical and growth objectives.

Similarly, in operations and project management, the effective coordination, monitoring, and completion of projects involve sound managerial skills. However, leadership qualities like vision and innovation become critical when projects hit inevitable roadblocks. Leaders find creative solutions and encourage a problem-solving culture, thereby enabling teams to adapt, learn, and grow from each challenge they face.

Customer relations and stakeholder management are further areas where management and leadership intersect. While managers ensure that customer service protocols are adhered to and stakeholder requirements are met, leaders go a step further by building relationships. They not only manage expectations but also inspire trust and confidence, turning customers and stakeholders into advocates for the business.

Innovation management is increasingly becoming a focal point in modern organizations. While traditional managerial roles may focus on maintaining existing processes and systems, the leader within is always searching for ways to do things better, faster, or more effectively. They are open to new ideas, encourage a culture of experimentation, and are not afraid to pivot when a chosen path proves unfruitful.

Communication, too, is a dual-responsibility function. Managers disseminate information, ensuring that everyone is on the same page, understands their roles, and knows the timeline. Leaders, however, use communication to motivate, create a shared sense of identity, and articulate a vision that others can rally behind.

The functions and responsibilities within modern organizations are increasingly calling for a hybrid skill set that combines the operational focus of management with the people-centered, forward-thinking attributes of leadership. Those who can integrate these dual aspects are likely to find themselves well-equipped to meet the multifaceted challenges that characterize today's dynamic business environment.

Specific Scenarios Where Leadership and Management Are Inseparable

To bring these abstract ideas to life, consider the role of a startup CEO. In the morning, they might be in a board meeting, defining the company's strategic vision. By afternoon, they could be reviewing quarterly budgets and signing off on resource allocation. They shift gears from inspiring the troops with motivational talks to troubleshooting operational bottlenecks. Such a role does not allow the luxury of being just a manager or a leader; it demands prowess in both domains.

Another illustrative scenario is that of a nonprofit organization grappling with a sudden loss of funding. The leader needs to reassure the team, realigning them to the organization's mission and reinvigorating their passion for the cause. At the same time, managerial acumen is required to revise the budget, reallocate resources, and maybe even spearhead a new fundraising strategy.

In these specific cases, and countless others like them, the two roles are not just interconnected; they are inextricably linked. Failing to recognize this leads to an incomplete, and therefore less effective, approach to solving the complex problems and challenges organizations face today.

As we navigate through this nuanced landscape, it becomes increasingly clear that the grey area is not a realm of confusion but one of enriched possibilities. This is where dynamic professionals and successful organizations often find themselves, not confined to the limitations of either role but empowered by the capabilities of both.

Understanding That Many Professionals Exhibit Both Leadership and Management Traits

As we dive deeper into the multifaceted nature of organizational roles, it becomes evident that the 'either-or' binary of being a leader or a manager doesn't truly capture the richness of professional life. The truth is many roles require a blend of both leadership and management skills for optimal effectiveness. Let's consider some prime examples and discuss the emergence of hybrid models that recognize this dual need.

Examples of Roles Requiring Both Skills

Middle management positions are perhaps one of the best examples of roles that require a healthy mix of leadership and management skills. These professionals often find themselves sandwiched between senior leadership and frontline staff, translating strategic goals into actionable plans. They need to inspire and motivate their teams (leadership) while simultaneously ensuring that daily operations align with broader organizational objectives (management).

Project managers, too, epitomize this duality. While they must meticulously plan, track, and execute projects (management), they are also responsible for rallying the team, resolving conflicts, and maintaining a cohesive vision throughout the project lifecycle (leadership).

In healthcare, roles like that of a chief nursing officer or head surgeon require not only a mastery of medical protocols and procedures but also the interpersonal skills to lead teams through high-stakes, often stressful environments.

Similarly, educational administrators, such as school principals or university deans, must balance curriculum management, staff oversight, and institutional compliance with the inspirational aspects of leading educators and students toward academic and personal growth. They must manage budgets and schedules while creating an atmosphere that fosters learning and encourages innovation and inclusion.

Chief Technology Officers (CTOs) in the tech industry are another prime example. They are responsible for both guiding the technological vision of a company (leadership) and overseeing the development and maintenance of technology solutions (management). The ability to lead tech teams innovatively while ensuring that projects are completed on time and within budget is a challenging task requiring both sets of skills.

Entrepreneurs, especially those in startups, often wear both hats out of necessity. They have to be visionaries who can inspire investors and early employees, while also being hands-on managers who can oversee everything from product development to marketing strategies and financial planning.

Non-profit executives also embody these dual roles. They must generate a passionate vision and mission to motivate volunteers and donors (leadership) while managing resources effectively to make a tangible impact (management). This balance is critical in organizations where the bottom line isn't just about profits, but also social impact.

Sales directors or managers have to meet targets and drive revenue (management) while inspiring their teams to be customer-focused and adapt to market changes (leadership). They must understand their products and the needs of their customers deeply and be able to communicate this understanding to their teams in a way that inspires action and commitment.

In the public sector, roles like city planners, police chiefs, and other governmental positions require the tactical skills to manage large teams and budgets, while also needing the leadership abilities to engage with the community and drive initiatives that align with broader societal goals.

Even roles that traditionally leaned more towards one skill set are evolving. For example, human resources professionals are no longer limited to administrative tasks like payroll and benefits management. They are increasingly seen as strategic partners in organizational development, contributing to leadership decisions and driving cultural change.

Therefore, across industries and sectors, there is an increasing recognition of the need for a blend of management and leadership skills. Professionals in roles that were once strictly about either oversight or vision are now expected to possess a nuanced mix of both, reflecting the complexity and interdependence of modern organizational challenges.

The Emergence of Hybrid Models in Organizational Structures

Recognizing the necessity for roles that encompass both leadership and management competencies, modern organizations are increasingly adopting hybrid models that deliberately blend these skill sets. For instance, some companies have introduced roles like "Lead Developer" or "Creative Director," where individuals are responsible for both doing and leading. These roles are crafted to ensure that technical expertise is coupled with team management and strategic planning.

Similarly, traditional hierarchy-based models are giving way to more agile, matrix, or flat organizational structures that require professionals to switch between managerial and leadership roles, often in the same day or even the same meeting.

Such hybrid models acknowledge that the most effective professionals are those who can flexibly adapt their approach to meet varying challenges. They understand that the keys to organizational success often lie in the overlaps, the intersections, the grey areas between traditional categorizations of leadership and management.

As we embrace this more nuanced understanding, we pave the way for professionals and organizations to break free from the constraints of rigid role definitions. It allows for a more dynamic, adaptable, and ultimately successful approach to tackling the multifaceted challenges that the modern business landscape presents.

The theoretical discussions about the blend of leadership and management traits have significant real-world ramifications. The impact of this harmonious integration is felt not just in organizational charts or strategic documents but in the daily grind of business operations, team dynamics, and corporate culture. Below, we delve into case studies that underscore the benefits of this integrative approach and examine the broad impact on performance and success.

Case Studies Demonstrating the Advantages

☐ A Tech Startup's Turnaround: In the fast-paced world of technology startups, one venture faced a stagnation phase despite a strong market presence. The CEO, initially a technical lead, adopted a more balanced role, merging leadership with management. He inspired the team to innovate (leadership) while also introducing data-driven decision-making processes (management). The result? A revitalized company culture and a 30% increase in quarterly revenue.

☐ Hospital Ward Efficiency: A chief nurse in a busy metropolitan hospital implemented a blend of managerial and leadership strategies to improve ward efficiency. By instilling a sense of purpose among staff members (leadership) and introducing a more effective scheduling system (management), patient satisfaction rates soared while staff burnout decreased.

☐ Manufacturing Excellence: A factory struggling with productivity issues turned its fortunes around when its floor manager adopted a dual approach. By fostering a culture of continuous improvement and teamwork (leadership) and implementing lean manufacturing principles (management), the factory saw a 20% improvement in productivity and a drop in defect rates.

When leadership and management are artfully balanced, the benefits ripple through every layer of an organization. On a team level, this results in employees who are not only more engaged but also more productive. They see the meaning in their work, motivated by the vision set forth by their leaders, while also appreciating the structural efficiencies that good management brings.

In terms of organizational culture, a harmonious blend fosters an environment of continuous learning and improvement. Employees feel empowered to take initiative, confident that there's a reliable framework to support them. This fosters a sense of ownership and accountability that is crucial for long-term success.

On a larger scale, the integration contributes to overall organizational success by allowing for quicker adaptation to market changes, more effective resource allocation, and a more aligned, cohesive strategy. Companies that excel in blending management and leadership skills are often the ones that dominate their markets, disrupt traditional business models, and set the standards for innovation and excellence.

In a nutshell, understanding and integrating the principles of both management and leadership isn't just an intellectual exercise; it's a practical imperative for contemporary success. With this holistic approach, organizations are better equipped to navigate the complexities of today's ever-changing business landscape.

As we wrap up this exploration into the overlaps between management and leadership, it's clear that recognizing and embracing these intersections is not merely a theoretical exercise. It is, in fact, a critical component for achieving real-world success in today's complex and fast-paced organizational environments. The delineation between management and leadership—though useful for academic distinction and initial understanding—is increasingly blurred in practice. Rather than being neatly compartmentalized, these roles often coexist, intertwine, and even feed off each other in symbiotic relationships that drive organizations forward.

For aspiring professionals and existing organizations aiming for excellence, adaptability, and long-term sustainability, taking a balanced approach is more important than ever. No longer can we afford to be just good managers or inspirational leaders; the demands of the modern world require a hybrid skill set that encompasses the best of both. As we've seen through case studies and real-world implications, those who manage to integrate both leadership and management traits are often more effective, more adaptable, and more capable of guiding teams and organizations to unprecedented heights.

Therefore, as you continue your journey in the professional world—whether you're at the helm of a multinational corporation, leading a small team in a startup, or anywhere in between—remember that the future belongs to those who can skillfully navigate the nuanced landscape where management meets leadership.

In doing so, you'll not only contribute to the immediate goals and bottom lines but also to the broader mission of creating a work culture that values both the visionary and the executor, the dreamer and the doer. And it is within this balanced culture that true excellence and innovation are born.

Chapter 5: The Distinctions: Key Differences and Why They Matter

In the preceding chapters, we thoroughly examined the definitions of management and leadership, their essential characteristics, and the roles they play within organizational structures. We also explored how these two seemingly separate disciplines often come together in practical situations, offering a richer, more complete approach to steering organizations toward their goals. While recognizing these convergences is crucial, it's equally important to acknowledge the distinct differences between management and leadership. A failure to do so not only muddles the understanding of these terms but also carries practical consequences that can affect an organization's performance in a myriad of ways.

In this chapter, our primary focus will shift toward these divergences. We'll examine why a nuanced understanding of the differences between management and leadership is more than an academic exercise—it's a practical imperative for anyone who aims to achieve both personal and professional success. With real-world examples, we will illustrate how misinterpreting or misapplying these terms can ripple through an organization, negatively affecting everything from employee engagement and morale to strategic execution and operational efficiency.

We'll also discuss how these concepts differ fundamentally in their approach to tasks, people, and goals. For instance, while managers may be more process-oriented, focusing on metrics and timelines, leaders often concern themselves with inspiring a shared vision among their team members. These differences, subtle or overt, can influence the tactics and strategies employed by organizations, affecting their competitiveness, adaptability, and ultimately, their long-term sustainability.

By offering guidance on how to balance the divergent aspects of these two roles, this chapter aims to provide you with the insights and tools needed to cultivate a working environment that not only fosters a culture of accountability and efficiency but also one of inspiration and continuous improvement.

As we delve into this complex but fascinating topic, you'll come to appreciate that understanding where management and leadership diverge is just as important as knowing where they intersect. It is this nuanced understanding that forms the foundation of truly effective organizational strategy.

Why the Correct Understanding and Application Matters

In any organization striving for excellence, the stakes for misunderstanding the roles of management and leadership are high. Let's start with the strategic importance of deploying the right approach at the right time. Managers and leaders both contribute to an organization's success, but they do so in different ways. Managers excel in situations that require stability and efficiency. Their role is indispensable when it comes to executing a well-defined strategy, optimizing processes, and ensuring that everyone is rowing in the same direction. On the other hand, leaders shine when an organization is navigating uncharted waters, needs to pivot its strategy, or is undergoing cultural transformation. Applying a managerial mindset to a situation that calls for leadership—or vice versa—can stall progress and dilute effectiveness.

Another critical dimension to consider is the impact on organizational culture and employee engagement. A managerial approach that focuses solely on tasks and processes, while neglecting the importance of human emotions and motivations, can lead to a toxic work culture. Employees might complete their assigned tasks but will likely do so without enthusiasm or creativity, which are often essential for innovation and long-term success. Conversely, an overly visionary leadership style that neglects the day-to-day operational aspects can result in a lack of focus and accountability, where beautiful ideas never translate into actionable reality.

Operational efficiency is another area that stands to be significantly impacted by the correct or incorrect application of management and leadership principles. Managers are typically responsible for streamlining operations, reducing waste, and ensuring that resources are used optimally. When the focus shifts too much toward visionary leadership without the balancing act of effective management, operational efficiency can suffer. Tasks may go uncompleted, deadlines might be missed, and resources could be squandered.

In summary, understanding when to employ management skills and when to apply leadership qualities is not just a theoretical debate; it's a practical necessity with real-world implications. It affects everything from the implementation of your strategic initiatives to the day-to-day morale and engagement of your employees, right down to your bottom line. Getting it right can set you on a path to success, while getting it wrong can send you veering off course, sometimes with dire consequences.

The Consequences of Misinterpreting or Misapplying the Concepts

The repercussions of misinterpreting or misapplying the concepts of management and leadership can be far-reaching, manifesting in a variety of detrimental ways within an organization. These pitfalls are not merely theoretical; they have been observed in real-world scenarios that underscore the necessity of clear understanding and appropriate application.

Take, for example, a case study of a technology startup that prioritized leadership attributes to the exclusion of sound management principles. While the charismatic CEO was able to inspire the team and attract investors with a compelling vision, the lack of operational expertise led to missed deadlines, overspending, and ultimately, the company's failure to deliver a viable product. The startup found itself hemorrhaging money and talent, leading to its eventual collapse.

Another illustrative example comes from the healthcare sector, where a hospital administrator, highly proficient in management but lacking in leadership skills, focused too much on cost-cutting measures. While operational efficiencies were achieved, the relentless focus on the bottom-line eroded staff morale and compromised patient care, tarnishing the hospital's reputation and leading to a decline in patient numbers.

In both instances, the absence of a balanced approach that integrates both management and leadership led to significant setbacks. The technology startup suffered from operational inefficiencies, and the hospital grappled with poor morale among its staff. Both organizations faced a decline in their reputations, which had a cascading effect on their prospects for long-term success.

But the consequences can extend beyond operational inefficiencies and employee morale. At its most extreme, a failure to properly balance management and leadership can even lead to organizational failure. Companies that navigate through crisis without adept leadership may never recover, while organizations that lack effective management can find themselves struggling with mundane but critical details, leading to financial decline and, eventually, bankruptcy.

In essence, the improper application or understanding of management and leadership concepts can be a costly mistake, undermining both immediate objectives and long-term goals. It can result in a range of problems, from operational inefficiencies and financial losses to poor employee engagement, low morale, and loss of reputation. In the worst-case scenarios, it can lead to the demise of the organization itself. Therefore, a nuanced understanding of these terms is not merely academic—it's a business imperative that holds significant consequences for the success or failure of any enterprise.

Key Differences Between Management and Leadership

The core distinctions between management and leadership, while subtle, have significant implications for how organizations operate and succeed. While both are essential for a well-functioning organization, they serve different purposes and require different skill sets.

At its core, management is about creating order and consistency. Managers excel in executing a vision, aligning people and resources to meet objectives, and setting up systems to measure success. They are the ones who ensure that once a course of action has been decided upon, all the pieces fall into place to make it happen. Managers excel at problem-solving; when they see a glitch in the system or a roadblock in the path, they look for practical ways to remove it.

Leadership, in contrast, is about setting that course in the first place. Leaders look beyond the how to the why. They inspire and motivate people, stirring their emotions and tapping into their aspirations. Leaders often challenge the status quo, seeking transformation and a new direction. They are not just solving problems; they are often identifying which problems are worth solving in the first place.

To illustrate these differences, let's consider a real-world scenario from a corporate setting. Imagine a company facing declining sales. A manager in this situation might look at the existing sales strategy, identify inefficiencies, reallocate resources, and introduce new performance metrics to reverse the decline. They would work to optimize the existing sales funnel, focusing on immediate issues like customer acquisition costs and conversion rates.

A leader, on the other hand, might approach the problem differently. They could question whether the company is targeting the right customer segments or even whether the product itself needs a revamp. They might propose a radical rethinking of the company's value proposition or explore entering an entirely new market. The leader would consider whether the decline in sales is a symptom of a deeper issue that requires a change in the company's strategic direction.

In an ideal world, these two approaches are complementary. The leader sets the vision and identifies new avenues for growth, while the manager executes this vision, making it a reality by aligning the team and resources appropriately.

So, while both roles are crucial, they are different in essence. Management often involves dealing with complexity—making sense of many moving parts and ensuring they fit together to achieve a goal. Leadership is about dealing with change—setting a direction, aligning people to it, and motivating them to overcome obstacles. Understanding these key differences is crucial for any organization that aims to thrive in today's complex and rapidly changing business environment.

Situational factors can influence whether management or leadership is more appropriate.

The role of context in determining the appropriateness of management or leadership can't be overstated. While we've discussed the key characteristics that differentiate managers from leaders, it's crucial to recognize that these roles are not static and can vary depending on a multitude of factors such as company culture, business stage, market conditions, and even individual project characteristics.

In a startup environment, for example, leadership qualities might take precedence as the company works to establish its market presence. The emphasis might be on vision, adaptability, and agility—traits often associated with strong leadership. In contrast, a well-established corporation operating in a stable market might emphasize management skills to optimize existing processes, maintain order, and gradually grow market share.

Even within the same organization, different situations can call for different approaches. During a crisis, for example, strong leadership is often required to navigate the organization through uncertainty and set a new course. On the other hand, once the direction is set, excellent management skills become crucial to execute the new strategy efficiently, aligning resources and overseeing the nitty-gritty details of implementation.

It's also worth noting that while some individuals may naturally excel more at management or leadership, situational factors can push them to adapt and grow into the other role as needed. For instance, a manager promoted to a C-level position may find themselves needing to adopt a more visionary style, even if their comfort zone is in the details and execution. Similarly, a leader may need to delve into the specifics when implementing a new strategic plan, requiring a managerial focus they haven't typically exercised.

The call for management or leadership isn't a one-size-fits-all decision but rather a situational one. Understanding the context in which you're operating can help you decide which set of skills to lean into, or whether a balanced approach might be more appropriate. This adaptability, powered by an understanding of the unique demands of each situation, is often the hallmark of the most effective leaders and managers.

Navigating the Balance

Sometimes the balance between management and leadership is akin to walking a tightrope. Too much emphasis on one over the other can lead to organizational shortcomings—be it a lack of vision and adaptability or operational inefficiency. However, finding that golden mean can significantly enhance both individual and organizational performance. Below are some tips and recommendations for professionals and organizations looking to strike this important balance effectively.

Firstly, self-assessment is crucial. Professionals should take the time to understand their natural tendencies. Are you more comfortable with planning and execution, or do you thrive in envisioning new possibilities and inspiring others? Knowing your strengths and weaknesses in both realms can help you identify what you need to work on to become a well-rounded professional.

Continuous learning is another key aspect. The landscape of business is always changing, and what worked yesterday may not be effective tomorrow. Keep yourself updated with the latest trends and theories in both management and leadership. Take courses, read widely, and don't hesitate to step out of your comfort zone to acquire new skills.

Also important is the need for emotional intelligence. Both managers and leaders require a high degree of emotional savvy to navigate the complexities of human behavior. Being aware of your own emotions, as well as those of your team, can guide you in determining when to take a managerial stance and when to inspire and lead.

Encourage cross-training within your organization. Allow your managers to take part in vision-setting exercises and give your leaders opportunities to engage with the practicalities of execution. This not only enriches the skill sets of both but also fosters a culture of mutual respect and understanding.

Remember, balance is not a one-time achievement but an ongoing process. Regularly review your approach and be willing to adjust as circumstances change. Whether it's a shift in organizational goals, a change in team dynamics, or a new external challenge, be prepared to reassess and recalibrate your balance between management and leadership.

Organizations, too, must foster environments where both management and leadership can thrive. This can be achieved through training programs, mentorship opportunities, and by setting clear expectations about the roles and responsibilities that come with different positions.

Effectively navigating the balance between management and leadership involves a constant cycle of self-assessment, learning, adaptation, and reassessment. Both individuals and organizations stand to gain immensely from this balanced approach, realizing benefits in operational efficiency, employee engagement, and the capacity for innovation and adaptation.

Chapter 6: Transitioning from Management to Leadership

The journey from being a manager to becoming a leader is often seen as a natural progression in one's career, but it's far more than just a title change or a new set of responsibilities. It represents a fundamental shift in how you approach your role within an organization, your team, and even yourself. This chapter is designed to serve as a roadmap for this pivotal career transition. As we explore this transformative journey, you'll not only learn what sets leadership apart from management but also discover the tools, mindset, and strategies needed to evolve successfully.

Understanding this transition is crucial for multiple reasons. First, as organizations grow and adapt to the rapidly changing business environment, the need for effective leadership becomes increasingly apparent. Managers are often the first in line for these leadership roles, given their experience and demonstrated ability in the organization. But being a great manager doesn't automatically make one a great leader. This chapter will delve into what needs to change, what needs to be learned, and how to navigate through common barriers that impede this transition.

Secondly, personal career growth often necessitates this evolution. As you move up the ladder, the very skills that made you an excellent manager may need to be augmented by leadership qualities you've not yet had to develop. How do you make this shift without losing the essence of what made you successful in the first place? We'll address this question comprehensively, equipping you with actionable advice and real-world examples.

Finally, organizations as a whole benefit when their managers can seamlessly transition into leaders. It fosters a culture of internal growth and stability, which is crucial for long-term success.

So, whether you're an aspiring leader or an organizational stakeholder interested in talent development, this chapter offers critical insights. It aims to demystify the transition, offering a blend of theoretical understanding, practical advice, and case studies that highlight the paths taken by those who have successfully made the leap. By the end of this chapter, you should have a robust framework to guide your transition from a capable manager to an inspiring leader.

The Natural Progression: Why Managers Often Become Leaders

In the hierarchical structure of most organizations, it's not surprising that managerial roles are frequently viewed as steppingstones to leadership positions. Managers, by the nature of their responsibilities, have a deep familiarity with the workings of their team and department, including challenges, capabilities, and how to achieve specific objectives. This intimate knowledge of organizational processes and personnel makes them ideal candidates for roles requiring broader oversight and strategic vision—traits commonly associated with leadership.

As one ascends the organizational ladder, the scope of influence and decision-making tends to expand. Early in a career, the focus is often technical and task oriented. Can you code efficiently? Can you close sales? Can you manage a project within its time and budget constraints? However, as you move into managerial roles, the focus shifts towards supervising others doing these tasks. You are evaluated not merely on your individual output but on your ability to ensure that your team is effective, coherent, and motivated. In essence, you start the transition from a 'doer' to an 'enabler.'

As you climb even higher, especially into executive roles, the questions asked of you change once more. Now, it's about setting direction and strategy. Can you inspire an entire division or even an entire organization to move toward a particular vision or objective? The stakes are higher, the impact is broader, and the skills needed are more complex. Leadership skills become not just beneficial but crucial.

There is also an increasing emphasis on emotional intelligence, strategic vision, and the ability to navigate ambiguity—traits that are more aligned with leadership than management. As the scale of responsibility increases, so does the complexity and unpredictability of challenges. Managing these challenges often requires not just the ability to oversee processes but to inspire a shared vision, engage in complex problem-solving, and bring people along in a journey of transformation.

Thus, it's not just that managerial roles are steppingstones to leadership roles; it's that the skill set, mindset, and even the types of challenges faced naturally evolve in a way that requires an increasing focus on leadership capabilities. This is why an understanding of the intricate relationship between management and leadership is so crucial for career growth and organizational success.

Skill Sets: What Needs to Change

The journey from management to leadership is not merely a change in title or an expansion of responsibilities; it is a transformative process that requires personal growth, learning, and skill acquisition. While managerial skills provide a solid foundation, aspiring leaders need to cultivate additional capabilities to navigate the complexities that come with leadership roles.

Many of the skills honed during one's managerial career serve as valuable assets when transitioning to leadership. Effective communication, for instance, is crucial in both roles. Managers need to articulate tasks clearly, provide constructive feedback, and liaise between their team and upper management. As a leader, this skill extends to influencing and inspiring your team, stakeholders, and sometimes even the public.

Similarly, problem-solving is another skill that is indispensable in both roles. Managers often use this skill to optimize processes, allocate resources, and overcome day-to-day challenges. Leaders, however, will find that the problems they face are more abstract, complex, and far-reaching. Therefore, the problem-solving skills acquired during management years will continue to serve leaders but in a more strategic context.

While the aforementioned skills will prove beneficial, they alone are not sufficient for effective leadership. One of the most critical skills a leader must possess that a manager may not need to the same extent is vision—being able to see the 'big picture' and guide the organization toward it. Vision is what sets the stage for innovation, inspiration, and forward strategic planning.

Emotional intelligence is another critical skill that needs to be finely tuned. While managers do require a basic level of empathy and social skills, leaders must excel in these areas. They should be adept at reading the room, understanding their team's motivations, and fostering an environment where people feel valued and inspired.

Risk-taking and decision-making also acquire a new dimension in leadership. Managers make decisions, but often within frameworks established by those above them. Leaders must make decisions that could change the course of the entire organization, often with incomplete information and high levels of uncertainty. The courage to make such decisions—and take accountability for them—is a skill that must be cultivated.

Resilience and adaptability are key leadership traits. Unlike managerial roles, where processes and guidelines provide some level of predictability, leadership often involves navigating uncharted waters. Being resilient in the face of challenges and adaptable when conditions change are vital for not just surviving but thriving in leadership positions.

The transition from management to leadership is less of a leap and more of an evolution, requiring both the refinement of existing skills and the acquisition of new ones. It's a complex yet rewarding journey that promises personal growth and the opportunity to make a lasting impact on your organization.

Mindset Shift: From Control to Empowerment

One of the most profound changes in transitioning from management to leadership is the psychological shift that occurs in how you approach your role and responsibilities. This mindset shift can be unsettling but is crucial for success in a leadership position. It involves moving from a mode of control to one of empowerment, and from an orientation centered around tasks to one focused on people and visions.

As a manager, your primary focus is often on control—ensuring that tasks are completed on time, resources are allocated efficiently, and projects stay within budget. The manager's realm is one of oversight, aiming to keep the team or department running like a well-oiled machine. However, leadership demands a transition from control to empowerment. Instead of merely directing processes and overseeing tasks, leaders are tasked with empowering their teams to be self-sufficient, innovative, and aligned with the organization's broader goals. The leader's role is to build a framework within which their team can excel, not to micromanage their every move.

Empowering your team requires trust and a willingness to let go of some of the control you were accustomed to as a manager. You need to equip your team with the tools, knowledge, and autonomy they require to solve problems on their own. This approach not only frees up your time for more strategic, big-picture thinking but also fosters an environment where team members can grow and excel.

Another key aspect of the mindset shift involves moving your focus from tasks to people and visions. While tasks are undeniably important, leadership requires a broader perspective. As a leader, your primary responsibility is to inspire and motivate, to set the stage for innovation and creativity. You are the custodian of the team or organization's vision, ensuring that every action and decision taken is aligned with this overarching objective.

This shift can be challenging because it involves intangibles that can be difficult to measure, unlike the concrete metrics often used in management. Success in leadership is often seen in the collective growth and satisfaction of the team, the innovation and improvements they bring, and how well they contribute to the achievement of long-term goals.

Therefore, the mindset shift from management to leadership is much more than a change in job description; it is a fundamental change in how you view your role and your team. You move from being a 'doer' to being a 'guide,' from a problem solver to a vision setter, and from a taskmaster to someone who empowers. It's a transformative experience that broadens your horizons and allows you to have a far-reaching impact on your organization.

Preparing for the Transition

Making the leap from a managerial role to a leadership position is a monumental career step, fraught with both challenges and opportunities. Therefore, it's crucial to prepare adequately for this transition. A thoughtful approach can significantly ease the shift, ensuring you're not just reacting to new challenges, but are strategically poised to handle them effectively. Here are some ways to prepare for this important career move.

One of the most valuable resources for anyone looking to transition into a leadership role is the guidance of a mentor. A mentor who has successfully navigated this path before can provide invaluable insights into what to expect, and how best to prepare for and handle the challenges that come with leadership. Mentorship isn't just about having someone to seek advice from; it's about learning from their experience, understanding the nuances of leadership, and even gaining a sounding board for your ideas and plans. A good mentor can help you avoid common pitfalls and offer wisdom that could take years to learn on your own.

There is an abundance of training programs designed specifically for developing leadership skills, ranging from workshops and seminars to comprehensive executive training courses. These structured learning environments can provide you with essential skills, from strategic thinking to emotional intelligence, which are key to successful leadership. A dedicated training program can also be a good opportunity for networking, allowing you to meet and learn from other aspiring leaders. While a training program demands an investment of both time and resources, the returns can be substantial and long-lasting.

Self-directed learning is another indispensable component in preparing for a leadership role. The most effective leaders are often those who are self-aware, continually seeking to improve and adapt. Books, academic papers, online courses, and even podcasts about leadership can offer a wealth of information. Make it a habit to learn continuously and stay updated with the latest trends and theories in leadership. Reflecting on these resources can help you internalize the kind of leader you aspire to be and plan the steps to get there.

The transition from management to leadership is not just a career step but a personal journey that demands careful preparation. Through mentorship, training programs, and self-study, you can equip yourself with the tools, perspectives, and knowledge you'll need to lead effectively. This multifaceted approach ensures you're not just moving into a leadership role but are growing into a leader in every sense of the word.

Barriers to Transition and How to Overcome Them

The journey from manager to leader can be a winding road laden with obstacles, many of which may not be immediately obvious. These barriers can stem from ingrained habits, organizational culture, or even from the fear of stepping into the unknown. Recognizing and understanding these challenges is the first step in overcoming them.

One of the most common obstacles that managers face when aspiring to become leaders is the constraint of their own mindset. Managers are often focused on tasks, deliverables, and timelines. This focus, while effective in a managerial capacity, can limit one's ability to inspire teams, cultivate innovation, and think strategically. Overcoming this barrier involves consciously shifting one's focus from the immediate tasks at hand to the broader objectives and visions of the organization. This doesn't mean abandoning attention to detail; rather, it involves expanding your scope of awareness and planning.

Another common issue is organizational resistance. Many organizations have a deeply ingrained culture that delineates roles strictly, making it difficult for managers to evolve into leaders. This can be addressed by becoming an advocate for change within the organization, starting with open conversations about the value of flexible roles and fluid transitions between management and leadership. Identifying allies within the organization and even seeking external case studies that demonstrate the efficacy of such transitions can help make your case more compelling.

A lack of self-confidence can often hold back potential leaders. The fear of failure, especially when venturing into unfamiliar territories of leadership, can be paralyzing. To counter this, it may be beneficial to engage in self-reflection, perhaps keeping a journal to note your progress, concerns, and any roadblocks you encounter. Self-affirmation and positive visualization can also go a long way in boosting confidence.

To overcome these challenges, proactive measures should be taken. Engaging in continuous learning, seeking out mentorship opportunities, and even undergoing formal leadership training can provide the necessary skills and insights to successfully make the transition. It's also essential to practice resilience and adaptability, as the journey will inevitably present unforeseen challenges that require quick thinking and agile problem-solving.

The barriers to transitioning from management to leadership are numerous but not insurmountable. With the right strategies, these challenges can not only be overcome but turned into steppingstones on your path to becoming an effective leader.

Case Studies: Successful Transitions

The transition from management to leadership is one that has been successfully navigated by many individuals across different sectors and industries. Understanding these real-world cases can provide valuable insights into what it takes to make such a transition smoothly and effectively.

One compelling example is that of Sheryl Sandberg, who began her career in various managerial roles, including serving as Vice President of Global Online Sales and Operations at Google. When she moved to Facebook as the Chief Operating Officer, her role underwent a significant shift. No longer was she just overseeing operations; she became a thought leader, author, and advocate for women in the tech industry. Sandberg's transition involved not just managing teams and tasks but also inspiring a whole generation of women to "Lean In," as her book suggests. One of the critical factors in her successful transition was her ability to adapt her communication skills from straightforward management directives to storytelling and advocacy, a hallmark of impactful leadership.

Another noteworthy example is that of Satya Nadella at Microsoft. Nadella served in a range of management positions within the company before becoming its CEO. Upon taking the reins, he immediately set a new vision for Microsoft, emphasizing a "mobile-first, cloud-first" world. His leadership was not just about maintaining the status quo but transforming an entire organization to meet the future. Nadella's capacity for strategic thinking, which he had honed in his managerial roles, served him well in defining a new path for Microsoft. However, what truly marked his transition into effective leadership was his focus on changing the company culture to one of learning and growth, a clear shift from mere management to inspirational leadership.

These successful transitions share common traits. First, both leaders were open to learning and took proactive steps to grow beyond their initial skill sets. Second, they demonstrated a distinct ability to change their communication styles to match their new roles, moving from direct, task-oriented communication to a more inspiring and visionary dialogue. Lastly, they both showed a willingness to adapt and to drive change, not just in their tasks but in the broader culture of their organizations. These traits did not negate their managerial skills but rather built upon them, proving that management and leadership could indeed coexist and even complement each other when appropriately applied.

Leadership Styles: Finding Your Own

When transitioning from a managerial role to a leadership position, one of the most vital shifts is adopting a leadership style that resonates not just with you but also with those you're aspiring to lead. Leadership style is more than just a buzzword; it's a composite of how you communicate, motivate, inspire, and guide others towards achieving common goals. It encompasses your method of problem-solving, your approach to conflict resolution, and the way you build a team culture.

There are numerous leadership styles, each with its own merits and shortcomings, and understanding these can help you find the one that aligns best with your personal values and the needs of your organization. Some popular leadership styles include the autocratic, where the leader has significant control over all decisions and little input from team members; democratic, where decision-making is distributed and team members are encouraged to share their opinions; transformational, focused on inspiring and transforming teams; and transactional, which relies on rewards and penalties to motivate team members.

Finding your leadership style isn't a matter of picking one from a list but involves a nuanced process of self-discovery and external feedback. Begin by reflecting on your interactions in various professional settings. How do you naturally communicate? What motivates you, and what seems to motivate those around you? How do you react under stress? These questions can offer valuable insights into your natural inclinations.

Experimentation is another crucial component in this journey. Don't be afraid to adapt different styles to various situations to see what works best. For example, you might find that a more democratic approach is effective in brainstorming sessions, whereas a more autocratic style might be needed when quick decisions are required.

Encouraging feedback is also key to refining your leadership style. Open lines of communication with team members, peers, and even mentors can provide you with different perspectives on your effectiveness as a leader. Listening to what others have to say and adjusting your approach accordingly is not a sign of weakness but of a mature, adaptive leader.

Your leadership style is an evolving aspect of your professional development. It's not set in stone, and it should be flexible enough to adapt to different challenges, opportunities, and team dynamics. Taking the time to reflect, experiment, and gather feedback will not only help you identify your most effective leadership style but also equip you with the adaptability that modern leadership demands. This adaptability can be a vital asset as you navigate the complex and often unpredictable waters of organizational leadership.

Assessing Your Readiness

Making the transition from management to leadership is a significant step, one that requires careful planning and introspection. You're not merely changing job titles; you're assuming a new set of responsibilities, adopting a new mindset, and, in many ways, influencing the direction of your team or even your entire organization. Given the magnitude of this shift, how can you be sure you're ready? Assessing your readiness involves both self-reflection and external validation, and there are various tools and metrics available to help you make this evaluation.

Firstly, there's self-assessment. Various psychometric tests and leadership readiness assessments can give you an initial gauge of your preparedness. These tests typically evaluate your emotional intelligence, strategic thinking capabilities, ability to handle stress, and your aptitude for inspiring others—attributes that are crucial for effective leadership. While no test can provide a full picture of your leadership capabilities, they offer a useful starting point.

Next, there's your track record. Have you successfully led smaller teams or projects? Have you been able to influence decisions at higher levels of your organization? Can you point to specific instances where your managerial competence positively impacted your team or project outcomes? Past behavior is often a good predictor of future performance, and a history of successful management can indicate potential for leadership.

Self-assessment and a good track record are just pieces of the puzzle. The external validation—feedback from peers, subordinates, and mentors—can provide invaluable insights into your readiness for a leadership role. While you might feel ready to lead, your team's perception is equally crucial. Regular performance reviews, 360-degree feedback, or even informal conversations can provide an external perspective. If those who have worked closely with you can visualize you in a leadership role and express confidence in your abilities, it's a strong indicator that you're ready for the transition.

Peer and mentor feedback can also help you identify areas for improvement, whether it's communication, emotional intelligence, or strategic planning. Mentors, with their greater experience, can offer particularly insightful advice. They can help you understand organizational complexities, manage challenging relationships, and navigate your career transition more smoothly. Their feedback can act as a compass, directing you toward the areas where you need development.

As we wrap up this chapter, it's worth revisiting the essential themes we've explored. Transitioning from management to leadership is not merely a promotion or a change in job title; it's a fundamental shift in mindset, responsibilities, and even identity. The stakes are high, and the journey is complex, but the rewards— both personal and organizational—can be immense.

We've delved into why managerial roles often serve as steppingstones to leadership positions, underscoring the organic progression often seen as one ascends the organizational ladder.

We've dissected the skill sets you'll need, some of which are transferable from your managerial experience, and others you'll have to cultivate anew. We've also discussed the critical mental shift from a focus on control to one of empowerment, a transition that is as psychological as it is operational.

The chapter has offered you a toolkit for preparing for this transition. From identifying potential barriers and ways to overcome them to considering mentorship and self-study, we've laid out actionable steps you can take to equip yourself for the journey ahead. We've even looked at methods for assessing your readiness, balancing self-evaluation with external feedback to give you a comprehensive view of your preparedness for the challenges of leadership.

But understanding these elements is just the first step; the real work is in applying this knowledge to your own career. This transition isn't something that happens overnight. It requires planning, continuous learning, and most importantly, a deep commitment to personal and professional growth. As you close this chapter, I encourage you not to see this as the end of your inquiry into what it means to move from management to leadership but rather as a starting point. Reflect on your own situation, seek feedback, and begin the hard yet fulfilling work of steering your career toward leadership.

Chapter 7: Striking the Balance: The Hybrid Leader-Manager

In an increasingly complex and rapidly changing business landscape, the roles of leaders and managers are evolving. Organizations are finding that the traditional silos that separated these roles are less effective in today's multifaceted operational environment. The demand for a new breed of professionals—those who can efficiently manage while inspiring and leading their teams—is on the rise. Welcome to Chapter 7, where we delve into the concept of the Hybrid Leader-Manager, a role that combines the best of both worlds.

The need for a hybrid role is more than just a trend; it's a response to real-world challenges. Whether it's navigating the complexities of global markets, driving digital transformation, or fostering a culture of continuous innovation, organizations require individuals who can harmonize varied skill sets. In this chapter, we explore the traits and characteristics that make up this new role, the advantages and potential pitfalls of adopting such a model, and the necessary steps for transitioning into a hybrid leadership-management capacity.

We'll also bring in case studies that provide living examples of successful hybrid leader-managers, detailing how they manage to juggle the responsibilities of both roles effectively. If you've been intrigued by the earlier discussions on the distinctions and overlaps between leadership and management, this chapter will offer you a compelling lens through which to view the future of organizational dynamics.

If you are a manager eyeing a more strategic role within your organization, or a leader wondering how to better execute your vision, this chapter holds vital insights for you. And for organizations looking to break down the traditional silos that separate leadership and management, embracing the hybrid role could well be a strategy for long-term success. Let's delve in and explore how you can become a Hybrid Leader-Manager in this era of change and opportunity.

The Rise of the Hybrid Role: A Necessity in Modern Business

The 21st-century organizational landscape is far more dynamic, complex, and uncertain than in decades past. Gone are the days when roles were rigidly defined and compartmentalized. Today's challenges require professionals capable of wearing multiple hats, seamlessly transitioning between roles to meet ever-changing demands. This has given rise to the hybrid leader-manager, an individual equipped with a blend of leadership vision and management acumen.

Several factors contribute to the emergence of this hybrid role, starting with technological disruption. In the digital age, change is rapid and often unpredictable. New tools, platforms, and digital ecosystems are continually emerging, requiring organizations to be nimble and adaptive. These changes don't just need management; they need leadership to steer the ship in a direction aligned with long-term strategic goals. Simultaneously, organizations can't afford to drift aimlessly in the name of innovation; they require the stability and efficiency that good management brings.

The need for the hybrid role is also being driven by the increasing complexity of global business operations. Companies are no longer limited by geographical borders; they operate on a global scale, managing diverse teams and serving multicultural customer bases. Navigating this complexity requires not only the ability to manage logistics, operations, and personnel effectively but also the capacity to inspire and unite people around a shared vision and culture.

Moreover, social shifts, such as the increasing importance of corporate social responsibility and ethical business practices, have put pressure on companies to be more than just profit-driven entities. This calls for leadership that can envision and champion such causes while managing the concrete metrics of business success.

Examples of Situations Where the Hybrid Role is Crucial

One area where the hybrid role is increasingly vital is healthcare, a sector characterized by rapid technological advances, regulatory challenges, and the need for compassionate caregiving. Here, professionals need to manage efficiently while leading with empathy and ethical considerations.

Startups are another domain where hybrid skills are often essential. A founder frequently starts as a visionary with a groundbreaking idea but soon realizes the need for strong management skills to translate that vision into a sustainable business model.

Even in traditional corporate settings, middle managers are finding that their roles are evolving. No longer can they act as mere conduits of executive orders; they are increasingly expected to contribute strategically and inspire their teams.

The modern business landscape is too nuanced, too dynamic, and too integrated for the traditional boundaries between leadership and management to exist in isolation. Thus, the rise of the hybrid leader-manager is not just an interesting development but a necessary evolution.

Characteristics of a Hybrid Leader-Manager: The Best of Both Worlds

The hybrid leader-manager is an individual who masterfully combines the strategic vision of a leader with the practical know-how of a manager. This creates a balanced skill set that allows them to navigate the complex and often ambiguous terrain of modern organizations. But what are the specific traits and skills that set the hybrid leader-manager apart? Let's delve into the characteristics that blend the best of both worlds.

Hybrid leader-managers are visionaries who can articulate a compelling future for their teams and organizations. They don't just focus on the "here and now"; they're able to look ahead, understand market trends, and set a course that aligns with broader organizational goals. This vision isn't confined to boardrooms; they are adept at communicating it in a way that resonates with everyone, from entry-level employees to stakeholders.

They don't stop at vision-setting. They are also pragmatists who understand how to turn that vision into reality. This requires a strong grasp of management fundamentals, from resource allocation and process optimization to performance measurement. They know how to break down larger goals into actionable steps and are committed to following through. Unlike leaders who may delegate the 'how' to someone else, or managers who may not concern themselves with the 'why,' hybrid leader-managers are actively involved in both.

Another striking characteristic is their emotional intelligence. They're not just focused on systems and processes but also on people. They understand that employee engagement, company culture, and team dynamics are not soft issues; they're crucial factors that impact the bottom line. Thus, they know how to manage people and lead them. They can give constructive feedback, foster collaboration, and build a culture of continuous improvement, all while inspiring loyalty and a sense of purpose among their team members.

One of the key skills of the hybrid leader-manager is adaptability. The ability to switch between leadership and management tasks as circumstances dictate is invaluable. For instance, in times of crisis, they may need to take on more of a managerial role to ensure stability and control. Conversely, during periods of stagnation or complacency, they might emphasize their leadership traits to drive innovation and change.

They excel in decision-making that integrates both short-term efficiency and long-term effectiveness. They're not swayed by quick wins or immediate gratifications. Instead, they assess situations from multiple angles, consider the implications of various options, and make decisions that align with both immediate needs and future aspirations.

The hybrid leader-manager is a multi-faceted professional who embodies a rich blend of characteristics from both domains. They're strategic yet practical, visionary yet grounded, and people-oriented yet process-focused. This blend enables them to guide their teams and organizations through the nuanced challenges of the modern business world, making them indispensable assets in any forward-thinking organization.

Advantages and Challenges: The Two Sides of the Hybrid Leader-Manager Coin

The concept of a hybrid leader-manager is becoming increasingly relevant in the ever-evolving business landscape. With their unique blend of skills, they are well-equipped to navigate the challenges of modern organizations. However, like any other role, the position of a hybrid leader-manager comes with its own set of advantages and challenges.

Advantages

One of the primary benefits of being a hybrid leader-manager is the ability to see both the forest and the trees; that is, they can focus on long-term visions while also managing the day-to-day operations that make those visions achievable. This comprehensive outlook can be particularly beneficial in dynamic environments where change is constant, and adaptability is key.

Another advantage is the efficiency that comes from a blended skill set. The hybrid leader-manager can smoothly transition between different types of tasks, from setting strategy to problem-solving on operational issues. This eliminates the need for a chain of command to move decisions up and down, thereby accelerating the decision-making process.

The emotional intelligence that characterizes hybrid leader-managers often leads to higher levels of employee engagement and satisfaction. They are adept at balancing the human element with the operational needs of the organization, fostering a work environment where employees feel valued, heard, and motivated to contribute their best.

Furthermore, they are often better equipped to foster innovation. With their understanding of both managerial constraints and the larger vision, they can provide their teams with the resources and space they need to think creatively while ensuring that such efforts align with the organization's objectives.

Challenges

However, the role is not without its challenges. The expectation to excel in both leadership and management can sometimes lead to role confusion, both for the individual and their team. A lack of clarity in when to employ which set of skills can lead to inconsistent decision-making and, consequently, reduced team confidence.

The breadth of responsibilities could potentially result in burnout. The hybrid leader-manager often has a longer list of expectations to meet, which might take a toll on their well-being if not managed carefully.

Not all organizational cultures or structures may be ready to support the blended role of a hybrid leader-manager. In strictly hierarchical or traditionally segmented organizations, there may be resistance to this holistic approach.

Mitigation Strategies

Addressing these challenges often involves clear role definition and setting appropriate boundaries. Time management and delegation skills become paramount to handle the diversity of responsibilities. Furthermore, regular training and skill updates are essential to maintain proficiency in both leadership and management tasks.

To avoid burnout, hybrid leader-managers would do well to adopt self-care practices and perhaps even consult with mentors who have successfully navigated the complexities of such a role. For the organizational challenges, advocating for the value of such a multifaceted role and demonstrating its benefits through small-scale successes can be ways to influence cultural shifts.

Transitioning into a Hybrid Role: The Roadmap to Becoming a Versatile Leader-Manager

In the modern, fast-paced business environment, the need for versatile professionals who can adeptly navigate both the realms of leadership and management is more pronounced than ever. Transitioning into a hybrid leader-manager role is a nuanced process that demands deliberate planning, strategic skill-building, and focused self-development. If you find yourself in a traditional management or leadership role and aim to evolve into this composite profile, the following insights could serve as a roadmap for your journey.

Necessary Steps for Transition

- ☐ Self-Assessment: The first crucial step is a thorough self-assessment to identify your existing skills, strengths, and areas that require improvement. Assess not just your technical abilities but also soft skills like communication, empathy, and strategic thinking. Various tools and assessment frameworks can help you gain a well-rounded view of your capabilities.

- ☐ Role Definition: Clearly outline what a hybrid role would look like in your specific organizational context. Discuss the possibility and parameters with superiors or human resources and gather their inputs on what skills and competencies are most critical.

- ☐ Gap Analysis: Based on your self-assessment and the defined role parameters, conduct a gap analysis to identify what skills or knowledge you lack. This gives you a targeted area for development.

- ☐ Skill Development Plan: Create a comprehensive skill development plan that addresses the identified gaps. This should include a timeline, resources needed, and specific milestones.

- ☐ Pilot Projects: Before fully transitioning, consider taking on small projects that allow you to exercise both leadership and managerial skills. The feedback from these initiatives can provide invaluable insights into your readiness and areas for refinement.

- ☐ Ongoing Review and Adjustment: Continuously assess your progress against the milestones set in your development plan.

Be prepared to adjust your plan as you gain more experience and as organizational needs evolve.

Training, Mentorship, and Other Resources

☐ Formal Training Programs: Various executive education programs focus on hybrid skills for modern leaders. These programs can offer theoretical frameworks, practical case studies, and even simulation exercises to prepare you for the role.

☐ Mentorship: Seek out mentors who have successfully navigated a hybrid role. Their experiences, insights, and advice can provide practical perspectives that are otherwise hard to come by.

☐ Online Courses and Webinars: The internet offers an abundance of resources to sharpen both leadership and managerial skills. Websites like Coursera, Udemy, or LinkedIn Learning offer specialized courses on everything from strategic visioning to operational efficiency.

☐ Books and Journals: A wealth of literature exists on both management and leadership. Regularly reading relevant books, journals, and articles can offer you both foundational theories and cutting-edge innovations in the field.

☐ Peer Networks: Join professional networks or online communities where you can discuss challenges, share insights, and learn from the experiences of others in similar roles.

☐ Feedback Mechanisms: Establish robust feedback mechanisms with your team and superiors to continually gauge your performance. Anonymous surveys, one-on-one interviews, and performance reviews can offer candid insights into your effectiveness in the new role.

Transitioning into a hybrid leader-manager role is a rewarding but demanding endeavor. The challenge lies in the balance—of skill, of time, and of responsibility. But with the right approach, commitment, and resources, this transition can not only be smooth but also be a significant milestone in your professional journey.

Case Studies: Success Stories of Hybrid Leader-Managers

The value of theory often comes to light when it's grounded in practical examples. To that end, the stories of individuals who have successfully stepped into the hybrid role of leader-manager can provide invaluable insights. These real-world cases illustrate how the amalgamation of leadership and management traits can result in transformative success, both for the individual and the organization.

Case Study 1: Transforming a Start-Up Into an Industry Leader

One of the most compelling examples is that of a young entrepreneur who co-founded a tech startup. Initially, her role was heavily managerial, focusing on day-to-day operations, resource allocation, and project timelines. However, as the company grew, she recognized the need for a more visionary approach to guide the organization into the future. Through ongoing learning and mentorship, she cultivated leadership traits like strategic visioning, inspirational communication, and a focus on organizational culture. Her balanced approach allowed the company to scale efficiently while also innovating, eventually becoming an industry leader. Key factors contributing to her success included her willingness to adapt, invest in continuous learning, and apply a balanced set of skills when tackling complex challenges.

Case Study 2: Revitalizing a Lagging Division in a Multinational Corporation

In another case, a middle manager in a multinational company was given the responsibility of a division that had been underperforming for several quarters. Historically a strong manager, he was skilled in process optimization and workforce management. However, these skills alone were insufficient to turn the division around. He decided to adopt a more leadership-oriented approach, inspiring his team through a newly articulated vision and encouraging innovation by challenging the status quo. Over time, the division's performance improved dramatically. A key contributing factor to his success was his recognition of the limitations of a purely managerial approach in a situation that demanded transformative change. By integrating leadership skills like visioning and inspiration, he was able to mobilize his team toward higher performance levels.

Case Study 3: Leading a Non-Profit to New Heights

In the non-profit sector, a director who had a background in social work found herself at the helm of an organization that was struggling financially. Her managerial skills were crucial in implementing more efficient processes that reduced costs. However, she also recognized that the organization needed a compelling narrative and vision to attract donors and volunteers. She began to develop her leadership skills, focusing on storytelling, public speaking, and strategic partnerships. Her dual focus on both management and leadership ultimately led the organization to financial stability and increased social impact. Key to her success was the ability to effectively juggle both short-term operational necessities and long-term strategic initiatives.

Factors Contributing to Success

Upon examining these cases, several common factors emerge that contributed to their success as hybrid leader-managers:

- ☐ Adaptability: Each was quick to recognize when a situation required them to pivot from their existing skill set, demonstrating remarkable adaptability.

- ☐ Lifelong Learning: An ongoing commitment to personal and professional development was evident, enabling them to continually broaden their repertoire of skills.

- ☐ Context Awareness: They were exceptionally good at reading the context in which they operated, understanding when to focus on process and when to drive change.

- ☐ Emotional Intelligence: In each case, high levels of emotional intelligence allowed them to navigate complex interpersonal dynamics effectively, a crucial trait in any leadership or managerial role.

- ☐ Balance: Perhaps most notably, each displayed a finely tuned sense of balance. They knew when to push and when to pull, when to manage and when to lead, and when to speak and when to listen.

These case studies underscore the idea that the roles of manager and leader are not mutually exclusive. Rather, they can be integrated into a complementary and powerful skill set that is increasingly becoming the hallmark of success in today's complex business landscape.

Leading and Managing: When to Use Which Skillset

Recognizing when to employ managerial skills versus leadership skills is a nuanced art that requires an in-depth understanding of situational context and the unique challenges at hand. It's less about strictly adhering to prescribed guidelines and more about developing an intuitive sense of what is required in any given circumstance. However, there are some broad indicators that can help guide you.

In crisis situations or when immediate action is required, managerial skills tend to take precedence. This is when operational acumen, decision-making speed, and the ability to guide processes efficiently come into play. On the other hand, when dealing with long-term strategic planning, fostering organizational culture, or initiating significant changes, leadership skills often rise to the forefront. In these situations, the ability to inspire, cast vision, and engage with people emotionally can make all the difference.

Let's consider a situational example to illustrate this. Imagine that a critical project is falling behind schedule and you're facing a looming deadline. This is a classic scenario where managerial skills are crucial. You'll need to quickly assess the situation, allocate resources efficiently, and perhaps even streamline some processes to meet the deadline. Once the crisis is averted, however, this might be an opportune time to employ your leadership skills by initiating a team discussion about what led to the crisis and how to prevent similar occurrences in the future. This is a moment to inspire the team and potentially change internal processes or culture for the long-term betterment of the organization.

This fluidity between managerial and leadership responsibilities is often what sets great leaders apart from good managers. It's not necessarily about completely switching from one mode to another but subtly adjusting the blend of skills to fit the situation. Knowing how to toggle between these two skill sets effectively is becoming increasingly important as organizational structures evolve to require a more integrated approach.

The concept of the hybrid leader-manager is more than just a trend; it's a response to the evolving complexities of modern organizational dynamics. We've delved into what defines this hybrid role, drawing upon its unique blend of leadership vision and managerial acuity. We explored the characteristics that make someone effective in this multifaceted position and examined both its advantages and challenges. We also provided guidance on how to transition into such a role, emphasized by case studies of those who have successfully navigated this journey.

The actionable steps outlined in this chapter serve as a roadmap for anyone aspiring to be more than just a manager or a leader. The idea is to cultivate a well-rounded skill set that allows you to be adaptable, resourceful, and effective, regardless of the situation at hand. Whether it's through mentorship, training, or conscientious practice, the aim is to prepare for a landscape that increasingly values this holistic approach to organizational leadership.

In closing, the call to action is straightforward but far from simple: embrace the hybrid role. In doing so, you're not just enhancing your own career prospects; you're contributing to a paradigm shift that has the potential to make organizations more agile, employees more engaged, and ultimately, businesses more successful. The hybrid leader-manager is not a stopgap or a compromise but a strategic response to the demands of modern business. By investing in the development of these composite skills, you're setting the stage for sustained personal and organizational success.

Chapter 8: Modern Implications: The Changing Landscape in the Digital Era

In today's rapidly evolving landscape, the influence of digital technology has become inescapable, altering every facet of our lives—from the way we socialize and consume information to how we work and conduct business. The digital era has not only changed our expectations but also redefined the way organizations operate, bringing with it a wave of opportunities and complexities. As we delve into Chapter 8, titled "Modern Implications: The Changing Landscape in the Digital Era," our focus shifts towards understanding these monumental changes and their impact on the roles of managers and leaders. This is not just another evolutionary step in organizational dynamics; it is a revolution that calls for a complete overhaul in our understanding of leadership and management.

The onset of the digital era, marked by advancements like the internet, cloud computing, artificial intelligence, and big data, has accelerated the pace of change like never before. Businesses that were once secure in their brick-and-mortar models are now either adapting or fading away, overtaken by more agile competitors that have effectively harnessed the power of digital technologies. With such transformative changes, the paradigms of management and leadership are also undergoing substantial shifts. The aim of this chapter is to offer a comprehensive examination of these shifts, unpacking the opportunities and challenges that come with them.

We will explore a range of key topics, from the evolving nature of managerial and leadership roles in a digital context to the ethical implications that arise with technological advancements. We will also delve into practical aspects like the essential skill sets required for the digital age and the rise of remote work. Through case studies, we'll illustrate real-world examples of both successes and failures in digital transformation, aiming to extract valuable lessons.

The objectives of this chapter are multifaceted. We seek to offer both a theoretical understanding and practical guidelines for navigating the digital landscape as a manager or leader. Furthermore, we aim to instill a sense of urgency for adaptation and continuous learning, which are no longer optional but essential for success.

The story of digital transformation is a sweeping narrative that encompasses various technological advancements that have reshaped the world as we know it. The journey can be traced back to the late 20th century, with the rise of the Internet. No longer were computers just isolated machines; they became portals to a new, interconnected world. This initial spark ignited a chain reaction of innovations, from the emergence of cloud computing, which decentralized storage and processing power, to the explosive growth of big data and artificial intelligence (AI), each compounding the capabilities of its predecessors.

Cloud computing brought forth an era of unprecedented scalability and flexibility, enabling organizations to access and store data remotely, dramatically lowering the costs associated with data management and operations. Big data technologies followed, allowing for the collection and analysis of vast amounts of information. Finally, AI has come into the picture, offering intelligent systems capable of learning and adapting, providing predictive insights, automating processes, and even interacting with humans in a sophisticated manner.

All these advancements have collectively redefined the speed at which organizations operate. Gone are the days when business cycles were long and drawn out. In the digital era, organizations can pivot almost instantaneously, responding to market changes and customer demands with lightning speed. This newfound agility has opened doors to novel business models that were unthinkable in a pre-digital world. Companies can now tap into 'Platform Economies,' where they act as facilitators rather than producers, or adopt a 'Freemium Model,' where basic services are offered for free while advanced features are monetized. The possibilities are seemingly endless, limited only by an organization's ability to innovate and adapt.

The implications for organizations in this digital age are profound. Speed and scalability are not just advantageous; they are prerequisites for survival. Companies can no longer afford to be slow-moving and rigid, as even a minor delay in decision-making can result in lost opportunities or a rapid erosion of market share. The new business models spawned by digital technologies are turning traditional strategies on their head, requiring leaders and managers to rethink how they create value.

The Evolving Roles in a Digital World

In the digital landscape, the roles of managers and leaders are undergoing a transformative shift that mirrors the broader changes in organizational structure and function. Traditional responsibilities are evolving, influenced heavily by the infusion of digital technologies that have permeated almost every facet of business operations.

For managers, the changes are manifold. They are now expected to not only manage people but also navigate sophisticated software tools for project management, human resources, and analytics. Digital dashboards replace paper reports, enabling real-time tracking of key performance indicators. Managing remote teams, a trend accelerated by global connectivity and the COVID-19 pandemic, has also become a new norm. This demands a more refined skill set that includes mastering digital communication tools and platforms. Managers must adapt to overseeing virtual teams, which requires different techniques for building team cohesion and ensuring productivity.

Leaders, too, are discovering that the cornerstones of good leadership such as vision, inspiration, and adaptability, must now be applied in a digital context. For instance, fostering an organizational culture of innovation is crucial for leveraging digital tools effectively. Leaders must be digitally literate, but they also need to inspire their teams to embrace continuous learning and stay updated with the latest technological trends.

As organizations adapt to the digital age, new roles are emerging that sit at the intersection of technology and traditional functional areas. Titles like Chief Digital Officer are becoming more commonplace, reflecting the need for executives focused solely on guiding digital strategy. Data Analysts are increasingly vital for interpreting the large sets of data that businesses collect, converting raw numbers into actionable insights. Agile Coaches are another addition, ensuring that the organization adopts flexible and efficient methodologies, originally rooted in software development but now applicable to a range of business processes.

These new roles often collaborate closely with traditional managerial and leadership roles, forming a hybrid structure that is more responsive and adaptive to rapid technological changes. In such a landscape, managers and leaders can no longer afford to work in silos or remain strictly confined to their traditional job descriptions. The digital age requires them to expand their horizons, continually update their skills, and work synergistically with specialists in new roles to ensure that the organization stays competitive.

The evolution of roles in the digital world signifies an organizational metamorphosis. This evolution is not just additive, supplementing old roles with new ones; it is transformative, changing the very way leaders and managers operate. With digital technologies offering unprecedented opportunities and challenges, the organizations that will thrive are those that adapt their leadership and management styles to the demands of this new frontier.

In today's digital landscape, the distinctions between traditional leadership and what is now being termed "digital leadership" have become markedly pronounced. While traditional leadership emphasizes broad qualities like vision, inspiration, and the ability to drive change, digital leadership hones in on a set of attributes that are specifically calibrated to the fast-paced, ever-changing digital environment.

Adaptability is perhaps the cornerstone of digital leadership. While adaptability has always been a valued trait, its importance is magnified in a digital context where market trends, customer behaviors, and competitive landscapes are in a state of continual flux. Traditional leaders often focus on setting a long-term vision, a course that may be charted out for years. Digital leaders, on the other hand, understand that such long-term plans need to be flexible and subject to iterative revisions based on real-time data and changing circumstances. The agile methodology, born in the world of software development, is now a strategy that digital leaders employ to manage change efficiently.

Openness is another key trait that distinguishes digital leaders. While traditional leadership may operate on a "need-to-know" basis when disseminating information, digital leadership recognizes the importance of transparency and the free flow of information. Open-source cultures, flat organizational hierarchies, and collaborative work environments are characteristic of organizations led by digital leaders. They value input from all levels of the organization, understanding that good ideas can come from anywhere and that collaborative effort often results in the best solutions.

Innovation is the third pillar of digital leadership. Traditional leaders may aim for steady, incremental improvement, emphasizing risk management and operational efficiency. Digital leaders, conversely, are almost entrepreneurial in their mindset, willing to take calculated risks in the pursuit of transformative innovations. This doesn't mean being reckless but rather having an appetite for experimentation. They understand that in the digital age, staying ahead often means being the first to leverage new technologies, methodologies, or strategies.

Now let's talk about the role of a digital leader in the context of an organization. Unlike traditional leaders who may delegate the specifics of digital strategy to IT departments or digital officers, digital leaders are intimately involved in shaping and driving digital strategy. They are not just figureheads who nod approvingly at technological initiatives; they are active participants in the digital transformation journey. They collaborate with digital experts but also possess enough digital literacy to ask the right questions, challenge assumptions, and guide the organization toward digital maturity. They act as evangelists for digital adoption within the organization, encouraging a culture that embraces rather than fears technological change.

Digital Management: Adapting Traditional Approaches

In the world of digital management, traditional approaches are undergoing a seismic shift, thanks in large part to the advent of advanced technologies that automate or enhance various managerial functions. While traditional management often involved a great deal of manual oversight—from tracking employee performance to managing project timelines—digital management allows for these tasks to be streamlined and, in some cases, automated, freeing managers to focus on more complex decision-making and strategy.

For instance, gone are the days when project management was solely about Gantt charts on paper and face-to-face status update meetings. Today, digital tools like Asana, Jira, or Microsoft Project allow managers to have real-time insights into project status, resource allocation, and even predictive analytics for potential bottlenecks. These tools don't eliminate the need for human judgment but do significantly augment a manager's ability to execute projects effectively.

Similarly, analytics, once a specialized skill, has now become part and parcel of a digital manager's toolkit. Platforms like Tableau or Google Analytics provide managers with the ability to quickly sift through large datasets and derive actionable insights, whether it's customer behavior patterns or employee performance metrics. What might have taken weeks of analysis in a pre-digital era can now be accomplished in a fraction of the time, enabling managers to react more swiftly to market trends or internal challenges.

Employee engagement is another domain experiencing digital transformation. Traditional methods like annual reviews are being complemented or even replaced by continuous feedback platforms that allow for a more dynamic and ongoing conversation between managers and team members. Tools for virtual collaboration, such as Slack or Microsoft Teams, are redefining what it means to be a "team" in the first place, breaking down geographical barriers and enabling new forms of collaboration that were previously unthinkable.

The digital landscape is not merely about using the latest tools; it's about a shift in mindset. Managers need to transition from being just operators to becoming savvy interpreters of technology. This entails not just knowing how to use a tool but understanding what questions to ask of the data it generates, or how to integrate different technologies to create new workflows or solutions.

Skills for the Digital Age

In today's fast-paced digital landscape, both managers and leaders need to arm themselves with a new set of skills that go beyond traditional business acumen. These skills can be broadly categorized into soft skills and technical skills, and they are essential for navigating the complexities of the digital age.

Starting with soft skills, adaptability emerges as a paramount quality. The speed at which technology evolves is staggering, leading to quick shifts in best practices, tools, and even entire business models. Managers and leaders must be able to adapt to these changes rapidly and guide their teams through the transitional phases, all while maintaining productivity and morale. This agility is not just about reacting to change but also about anticipating it. Those who can foresee industry trends or technological disruptions have a distinct advantage, allowing for proactive rather than reactive strategies.

Continuous learning is another soft skill that has become crucial. The half-life of skills is shrinking, which means what you know today may become obsolete sooner than you think. For this reason, both managers and leaders should cultivate a love for learning, not just for themselves but also within their teams. This could involve formal education, like courses and certifications in emerging fields, or informal routes like webinars, workshops, or self-driven research. The willingness to update and upgrade one's skill set is vital for survival in the digital era.

On the technical side, data literacy stands out as an indispensable skill. Data is often touted as the new oil, and for a good reason. It fuels decision-making and strategy, but only if one knows how to refine and make sense of it. Managers and leaders don't need to be data scientists but should understand how to interpret data correctly, ask the right questions, and make data-informed decisions. This extends to knowing how to use data analytics tools and platforms, as they are the instruments that translate raw data into meaningful insights.

Another technical skill that is gaining prominence is cybersecurity awareness. With the increase in remote work and the proliferation of digital platforms, security risks have escalated. Managers and leaders must understand the basics of cybersecurity, not only to protect organizational assets but also to instill a culture of security awareness within their teams.

The rise of remote work has been a significant shift in the professional landscape, further accelerated by global events such as the COVID-19 pandemic. This development has had profound implications for both managerial and leadership roles. The physical office, once the epicenter of work interactions and team cohesion, has been replaced by virtual meeting rooms, asynchronous communication platforms, and cloud-based collaborative tools. In this new environment, both managers and leaders face unique challenges and opportunities.

When it comes to managerial roles, remote work introduces variables that were either non-existent or less prominent in a traditional office setting. For example, ensuring that everyone is working efficiently requires different kinds of monitoring and evaluation mechanisms, given the absence of physical oversight. Managers must now turn to digital tools that track productivity and engagement, but without creating a culture of surveillance. The balance is delicate; the focus should be on outcomes rather than constant monitoring of activities. This new reality also means that managers need to think creatively about how to foster team cohesion. Virtual team-building activities, regular one-on-one check-ins, and consistent communication via digital platforms can go a long way in keeping the team united and engaged.

Leadership in a remote environment also undergoes a transformation. The leader's role in inspiring and motivating the team becomes even more critical when face-to-face interactions are rare. Setting a vision and keeping everyone aligned with that vision requires more than just a quarterly all-hands meeting.

Leaders must be adept at using digital communication tools to maintain a continuous presence among their teams. They need to be skilled at virtual storytelling, creating narratives that resonate and inspire even when delivered through a screen. Additionally, leaders should be the champions of a remote-friendly culture, setting the tone for work-life balance and asynchronous communication, which are often integral aspects of remote work.

Strategies for maintaining team cohesion and productivity in a remote setting are manifold. Managers may find it beneficial to establish 'rituals' that replace the watercooler conversations of a physical office. These could be weekly virtual team lunches, daily stand-ups, or regular 'ask me anything' sessions to facilitate open communication. Likewise, leaders could set up quarterly virtual retreats that focus on strategic planning and team alignment, incorporating both business and fun elements to foster engagement.

For both managers and leaders, emotional intelligence becomes incredibly important in a remote setting. Being sensitive to the challenges team members may face—such as isolation, distraction, or burnout—and addressing these proactively can make a significant difference. It could be as simple as sending a care package, as thoughtful as providing mental health resources, or as strategic as redesigning workflows to prevent fatigue.

The rise of remote work is not merely a logistical change but a fundamental shift in how organizations operate. Managers and leaders who understand the nuances of remote work, and who can adapt their styles and strategies accordingly, will be well-positioned to guide their teams toward success in this new normal.

Chapter 9: Case Studies: Real-Life Applications of Management and Leadership

In the labyrinth of organizational behavior and development, theory often falls short of capturing the intricate reality that professionals face. We've delved into the nuanced characteristics of both management and leadership, parsed through their similarities and differences, and even considered how these roles are evolving in the digital era. Now, we arrive at the nexus of theory and practice: real-world case studies that illuminate the complex dynamics and challenges of management and leadership. Welcome to Chapter 9, where we transition from abstraction to application, showcasing how the principles we've discussed thus far come to life in various organizational settings.

The value of case studies lies in their ability to synthesize complex theoretical constructs into relatable narratives. Through these narratives, the abstract becomes concrete, and the guidelines and strategies we've discussed can be seen in action, replete with the outcomes they produce. Whether it's a tech startup facing a pivot, a non-profit aiming to expand its reach, or a government project aiming for efficiency and impact, these case studies are designed to provide a multi-faceted view. We will look at the managerial and leadership approaches employed, scrutinize the decision-making processes, and evaluate the results to extract valuable lessons.

This chapter aims to be more than just a collection of stories; it seeks to be a lens through which you can reevaluate your own approach to management and leadership. For each case, we will dissect the context, the challenges faced, the strategies employed, and the outcomes achieved. But beyond the 'what' and the 'how,' we will also delve into the 'why'—the underlying principles that guided the actions of the individuals involved.

In the end, the goal is not just to appreciate the complexities and challenges inherent in these roles but to arm you with actionable insights. Whether you're a seasoned executive, a middle manager, or an aspiring leader, these real-world examples offer invaluable lessons that can inform your own journey.

Case Study 1: Turnaround at a Tech Company

In the fast-paced environment of the technology sector, companies can swiftly find themselves in precarious situations if they don't adapt and innovate. Our first case study delves into a tech company on the brink of failure, struggling with plummeting revenue, a disengaged workforce, and a product line that had lost its competitive edge. The board of directors, aware of the impending crisis, brought in a new CEO to turn things around. This is a gripping tale of how the interplay between sound management and inspired leadership can rescue an organization from the brink and set it on a new path toward growth and sustainability.

The tech company in question had several red flags that demanded immediate attention. First, there was the eroding market share; competitors had overtaken them in areas where they had once been pioneers. Next, the internal culture was characterized by low morale and a lack of motivation, exacerbated by poor financial performance and lack of direction. The final straw was a flawed product strategy that was neither aligned with consumer needs nor able to exploit emerging technologies effectively.

Management Actions: Strategic Changes, Layoffs, Restructuring
Once on board, the new CEO wasted no time and initiated immediate changes. The focus was on stabilization, which meant making some hard decisions like layoffs and pausing non-essential projects to conserve resources. By consulting with the board, stakeholders, and senior management, the CEO initiated a comprehensive restructuring plan that included the revamping of

the company's product line and a realignment of its market positioning. At the operational level, processes were streamlined to cut costs, improve efficiency, and increase responsiveness to market changes.

While the CEO's managerial actions were critical, the leadership dimension was equally compelling. Recognizing that no turnaround could be successful without the full commitment of the workforce, the CEO engaged in open dialogues with employees at all levels. Town halls were conducted where a new vision was laid out, one that connected with the company's original innovative spirit but also adapted to the current market needs. This was not just a vision cast from the top but one that was developed collaboratively, taking into account the perspectives and suggestions of those who would be responsible for its realization.

To boost morale and initiate a cultural shift, several initiatives were launched, including mentorship programs, recognition systems, and professional development opportunities. The CEO made it a point to champion these initiatives personally, thereby signaling their importance to the entire organization.

The company's journey wasn't without its bumps, but over time the results began to show. Market share slowly clawed back, employee engagement scores improved, and most notably, the restructured product line began to gain traction. The financials improved as well, signaling a return to stability and the promise of future growth. What can we learn from this case study? For one, it illustrates the power of combining effective management with transformative leadership. While the CEO's managerial actions were essential for stabilizing the company and setting a new course, it was the leadership actions that infused the organization with renewed energy and purpose. The case also highlights how management and leadership are not mutually exclusive but are complementary forces that, when applied skillfully, can navigate an organization through the most challenging circumstances.

Case Study 2: Non-Profit Growth

In stark contrast to the tech world, non-profit organizations operate with different objectives and constraints, but the necessities of skilled management and visionary leadership remain constant. Our second case study turns our attention to a non-profit organization with ambitious plans for expansion. Operating in the field of educational support for underprivileged communities, the organization had hit a plateau in both its reach and impact. However, under new guidance, the organization not only managed to expand but did so while strengthening its community bonds and ensuring long-term sustainability. This is a tale of how prudent management coupled with passionate leadership can make a real difference, even when resources are scarce.

This non-profit had a strong initial start but had recently encountered limitations in both fundraising and reach. The mission was noble: to offer educational opportunities to communities where such prospects were limited. However, they had only been able to operate in a handful of locations, and their funding sources were drying up. Adding to the complexity was a staff of devoted but largely untrained volunteers. It was clear that while passion was abundant, a more structured approach was necessary for the planned expansion to succeed.

The organization's new director, coming in with both corporate and non-profit management experience, immediately set to work on a strategic plan. Understanding the financial constraints, one of the first steps was to overhaul the budgeting process to align more closely with the organization's priorities and needs. New protocols were instituted for resource allocation, making sure that every dollar spent would contribute to meaningful outcomes.

Perhaps the most critical managerial move was to build partnerships. The director leveraged existing connections and created new alliances with local businesses, educational institutions, and other non-profits. These partnerships provided a range of benefits from financial sponsorship to volunteer staffing and in-kind donations, each contributing to the organization's goals.

While those managerial actions set the stage for expansion, it was the leadership activities that truly catalyzed growth. The director invested significant effort in community engagement, holding regular open forums, and actively listening to the concerns and suggestions of community members. This engagement was not just lip service; changes were made based on the community's feedback, building a much more participative and inclusive model.

The director was adept at stakeholder relations, consistently communicating with not just the community but also with volunteers, staff, and partners. Transparency and open dialogue helped foster an atmosphere of trust and shared purpose, essential attributes for any non-profit organization.

Within a couple of years, the non-profit had more than doubled its reach and increased its funding through multiple channels, including grants, partnerships, and community donations. More importantly, the quality of the educational programs improved, as evidenced by feedback and various success metrics.

The organization's transformation serves as an excellent example of how managerial skills can set the operational framework for success, while leadership skills can inspire and mobilize people toward a shared vision. It teaches us that whether in a corporate setting or a mission-driven non-profit, the tandem of sound management and inspired leadership can indeed move mountains.

Case Study 3: Government Project

The third case study provides an intriguing look into the realm of public service, specifically focusing on a government project with a diverse set of stakeholders. Unlike the corporate or non-profit sectors, government projects often present a unique set of challenges, including regulatory constraints, political considerations, and public scrutiny.

This particular project was aimed at modernizing public transportation within a large metropolitan area. A long-overdue endeavor, it required significant coordination among various city departments, contractors, and community organizations. From the outset, the sheer scale and complexity of the project called for an impeccable standard of management. Everything from procurement processes to construction timelines needed to be tightly coordinated to prevent costly delays and overruns. Ensuring compliance with an array of federal and local regulations was yet another critical task that fell squarely within the managerial domain. While the project had several logistical challenges, they were largely overcome through meticulous planning, effective resource allocation, and ongoing coordination among involved parties.

But it was in the leadership arena where the project faced its most formidable obstacles. Navigating the politics of public opinion and bureaucratic resistance required a special kind of leadership. The project lead had to venture beyond the scope of mere management and adopt a forward-thinking approach to bring disparate parties into alignment. Community meetings were held to garner public support, and relationships with key politicians were cultivated to secure essential political backing. Through the process, long-term goals were carefully framed to resonate with a wide range of stakeholder interests, thereby generating momentum that surpassed the constraints of short-term political cycles.

The project, while experiencing several delays and budget adjustments, was ultimately deemed a success. It not only modernized the city's transportation infrastructure but also led to several unexpected positive outcomes, including the creation of new jobs and community development initiatives.

The lessons here are manifold but underscore the indispensable roles of both management and leadership in complex, multi-stakeholder environments. While management skills were critical for ensuring that the project stayed on track logistically, it was leadership that guided it through the maze of political and social complexities. Both were essential in navigating the myriad challenges that arose, and their effective application led to a successful outcome that benefitted a broad spectrum of stakeholders.

Case Study 4: Small Business During the Pandemic

The COVID-19 pandemic presented an existential challenge for businesses of all sizes, but perhaps none felt the strain as acutely as small businesses. Our fourth case study zooms in on a small family-owned restaurant struggling to stay afloat as lockdowns and public health mandates upended its business model. The challenges were overwhelming: plunging revenues, uncertain employees, and a radically altered business landscape.

On the management side, immediate actions were necessary to cut costs and adapt to the new reality. This included reducing operating hours, renegotiating leases, and sadly, laying off some staff. The business also had to quickly implement remote work solutions for administrative staff and pivot to a take-out and delivery model to comply with public health guidelines. These were difficult but necessary managerial decisions aimed at sustaining the business through the immediate crisis.

However, this situation also called for extraordinary leadership. The business owner took the helm in crisis management, being transparent about the challenges while also motivating the team. Rather than merely managing the crisis, they led their employees through it. This involved a plethora of actions ranging from mental health check-ins to providing resources for remote work setup. The owner also managed to negotiate better terms with suppliers and even secured a small business loan to cushion the financial blow. They maintained a sense of community among employees through regular virtual meetings where everyone could voice their concerns and suggestions. The owner's empathetic and transparent approach fostered a sense of unity and common purpose among the team, which was crucial for morale during such an uncertain period.

The outcome of these combined efforts was survival and adaptation. While the business couldn't operate as it did pre-pandemic, it found new ways to generate revenue through online sales and takeout services. It also deepened its relationship with the local community by participating in food drives and other charitable endeavors, thus turning a crisis into an opportunity for enhanced community engagement.

Key insights from this case study highlight the necessity for both strong management and visionary leadership, especially during times of crisis. While managerial skills helped the business navigate immediate obstacles and implement practical solutions, it was leadership that kept the team united and focused on long-term sustainability. The agile adaptation to an unprecedented crisis demonstrated the importance of balancing both roles effectively to navigate complex challenges.

Case Study 5: Healthcare Sector

In our fifth case study, we turn our attention to a healthcare provider grappling with the inevitable but complex process of modernization. Located in a rapidly growing metropolitan area, the hospital faced rising patient numbers and an antiquated operational system. Challenges included outdated medical record systems, inefficient patient-flow procedures, and an overall lack of technological adoption that hindered both patient care and operational efficiency.

On the management front, the focus was to streamline operations and adopt technology. An electronic medical records system was implemented to replace paper records, saving both time and resources. Outdated medical equipment was upgraded, and logistical workflows were optimized to handle a higher volume of patients more effectively. These management actions, including budgeting for the new technologies and overseeing the timelines for their implementation, had immediate impacts on operational efficiencies.

However, technological and procedural changes alone wouldn't suffice; the human element had to be considered, which is where leadership came into play. The healthcare provider's top executives and medical directors took the initiative to ensure that the staff were not just informed about the changes but were active participants in the transition. A series of training programs were designed to help employees at all levels become proficient in the new systems. Additionally, a culture of continuous improvement was fostered, encouraging staff to give feedback and contribute ideas for ongoing refinements. Leadership actions extended to enhancing relationships with patients as well, with hospital leaders taking an active role in community engagement to understand the ever-changing needs of the patient population they served.

The results of this balanced approach were transformative. Patient care saw notable improvements, as reflected in patient satisfaction surveys and a decrease in treatment errors. Operational efficiency also received a boost, resulting in shorter waiting times and improved resource allocation. The hospital was even able to expand its services to offer new types of care, all while running more efficiently than before.

This case study serves as a compelling example of how effective management and visionary leadership can work hand in hand to achieve significant transformation. Management's role in implementing technological and operational changes was crucial for meeting the immediate needs of the healthcare provider. However, it was leadership that steered the cultural and human factors that ultimately determined the project's long-term success. Both roles were indispensable in their own right, yet their coexistence proved synergistic, producing results that neither could have achieved alone.

Case Study 6: Educational Institution

In the final case study, we focus on an educational institution dealing with declining enrollment numbers. The challenge was multi-faceted: not only were fewer students applying, but the academic achievements of the institution were also slipping, causing concern among faculty, students, and alumni.

To address the immediate issue of declining numbers, management sprang into action with a two-pronged approach. First, a comprehensive marketing campaign was designed to target potential students, showcasing new curricular developments and campus facilities. Second, curriculum adjustments were made to reflect more current and in-demand fields of study, in the hope that this would attract a broader range of applicants.

Addressing the issue at its roots required a broader strategic vision, which is where leadership stepped in. The institution's leaders identified a need to differentiate the school by offering unique educational experiences that could not be easily replicated by competitors. This included the development of specialized research programs, unique community-based learning opportunities, and a focus on interdisciplinary studies. To sustain this new direction, a vigorous alumni engagement program was also initiated, aimed at both reconnecting with the institution's community and fostering financial support for these new initiatives.

The outcomes of these combined efforts were multi-dimensional. In terms of enrollment, the institution not only halted the decline but began to see modest year-over-year growth. Academically, new and innovative programs led to increased student engagement and higher levels of achievement, further boosting the institution's reputation. The alumni community became more engaged and contributed financially at higher levels than in previous years, providing additional resources for research and scholarship opportunities.

This case study exemplifies how management and leadership, though different in function and focus, can combine to address both immediate and long-term challenges effectively. Management's role in updating the curriculum and implementing a targeted marketing strategy dealt with the urgent enrollment issues, while leadership provided the long-term vision that would make the institution relevant and competitive in the educational landscape. Once again, the co-existence and cooperation between management and leadership were not just beneficial but essential for success, underscoring the core theme that runs through all these case studies and indeed this entire book.

Analysis and Synthesis Across the Cases

In this analysis and synthesis section, we aim to knit together the various threads that run through the six diverse case studies. Despite the differences in sector, scale, and specific challenges faced, some common themes emerge that are instructive for both current and aspiring managers and leaders.

In each case, the need for both managerial competence and strong leadership is evident. Management provides the structural foundation, making strategic decisions about resources, time, and personnel to address immediate issues. On the other hand, leadership serves to give the organization its direction and ethos, making broader strategic choices that shape the institution in the long term. Neither can stand alone; the tech company needed structural changes as much as it needed a morale boost, and the educational institution needed both a fresh marketing approach and a renewed strategic vision.

The case studies show that the application of management and leadership can be highly varied depending on the context. For instance, in the tech and healthcare sectors, technology adoption and process optimization were crucial managerial tasks, while the non-profit and educational institution had a more significant focus on community and stakeholder engagement as part of their leadership strategy.

Each case study presented its own set of unanticipated challenges—be it the external shock of a pandemic for the small business or the complex politics in the government project. What stands out, however, is the flexibility and adaptability with which these challenges were met. Management often had to pivot— reallocating resources, adjusting timelines, or revising strategies on the fly. Leadership had to navigate through uncertainty, maintain team morale, and sometimes even redefine long-term goals to adapt to a changing reality.

In summary, the case studies collectively underscore the importance of having a balanced approach to management and leadership. They illustrate the need for organizations to be agile, adaptable, and prepared for the unexpected. While managerial skills set the stage for handling immediate challenges, leadership is what guides an organization through change and inspires teams to perform at their best. Recognizing when to manage and when to lead is not just a skill but an art that can have a significant impact on the success or failure of any venture.

Key Takeaways

The key takeaways from these case studies offer a wealth of practical insights for anyone aiming to refine their managerial or leadership skills, or for organizations looking to strengthen their teams. Here are some overarching lessons:

☐ Balance is Essential: An effective organization needs both strong management to handle the logistics, resources, and day-to-day operations, as well as inspirational leadership to set the vision, motivate the team, and steer the long-term course. A lack in either area can result in organizational shortcomings or even failure.

☐ Context Matters: The case studies reveal that management and leadership are not one-size-fits-all endeavors. The sector, scale, and specific challenges faced by an organization can dictate which skills are most crucial at any given time. Being attuned to the unique needs of your organization or project can make all the difference.

☐ Adaptability is Key: In an ever-changing environment, the ability to adapt is invaluable. Challenges, whether anticipated or not, will inevitably arise. How these are managed or led through can have significant ramifications for the outcome of any project or the health of an organization.

☐ Use of Technology: As seen in the healthcare and tech sector cases, keeping up with technological advancements is not optional. Both leaders and managers need to embrace digital tools, not just to improve efficiency but to stay competitive.

☐ Human Element: Whether it's a small business struggling through a pandemic or a sprawling government project, the human element remains critical. Leaders and managers must focus not only on strategy and resources but also on the morale, well-being, and professional development of their teams.

As you consider the trajectory of your own career or ponder the needs of your organization, these takeaways offer a framework. For those in managerial roles, consider how you might also embody leadership qualities to inspire your team and affect lasting positive change. If you're in a leadership position, don't overlook the importance of good management practices to keep the ship steady.

Conclusion: The Future of Leadership and Management

As we come to the final chapter of this comprehensive exploration into the intricate worlds of leadership and management, it's worth pausing to reflect on the extensive ground we've covered. From the origins and evolution of leadership to the modern implications of managing and leading in a digital age, we have delved into various facets that define and differentiate these vital organizational roles. This concluding chapter serves not merely as an epilogue but as a forward-looking lens, casting its gaze upon the rapidly evolving landscapes of business, technology, and society, to anticipate what the future may hold for leadership and management.

The pace of change is unrelenting. Globalization, technological advancements, demographic shifts, and a heightened emphasis on corporate social responsibility are just a few of the dynamic forces sculpting the realms of leadership and management. As we venture further into the 21st century, these roles are poised to become even more complex and interdependent, requiring a new set of skills, perspectives, and strategies. The metamorphosis is so seismic that what may have been considered best practices a mere decade ago could now be deemed obsolete. And as we grapple with an increasingly interconnected world replete with its own set of opportunities and challenges, the need for adept leaders and managers—those who can not only adapt to change but drive it— has never been more critical.

In the chapters that follow, we will explore these critical shifts and transformations, helping you prepare for a future that promises to be as challenging as it is exciting. Whether you're an aspiring leader, a seasoned manager, or a scholar keenly interested in the dynamics of organizational success, this chapter will equip you with a nuanced understanding of what lies ahead. We'll dissect the latest trends, ponder their implications, and offer actionable insights for how both individuals and organizations can best position themselves for the uncertain yet promising years to come.

By casting this spotlight on the future, our aim is to forge a bridge between the theoretical and the practical, the academic and the applied, and the past and the imminent. Through this, we hope to encourage not just understanding, but action, prompting you to apply what you've learned in innovative, impactful ways. After all, the future of leadership and management is not some distant realm to be discussed and observed from afar; it is a living, evolving entity that we all have a stake in shaping. So, let's embark on this final leg of our journey with an eye toward the opportunities and possibilities that await us.

The Impact of Globalization

Globalization has significantly transformed the way businesses operate, and its impact on leadership and management is profound. In a world where markets are increasingly interconnected, leaders and managers must grapple with a multitude of complexities, from navigating different cultural norms and expectations to managing geographically dispersed teams. The interconnected global economy means that events in one part of the world can reverberate in another, necessitating a level of global awareness and responsiveness that was not as pressing in previous eras.

Global reach also affects strategic planning. Leaders are now responsible for steering their organizations through both domestic and international opportunities and challenges. Global market trends, trade policies, and international regulations have become key considerations when setting organizational direction. Managers, too, are called upon to implement these strategies on a global scale, coordinating efforts across different time zones, languages, and cultural contexts. Human resource management is another area profoundly affected by globalization. The push for diversity and inclusion in the workplace is partly a response to globalization, reflecting the need for a workforce that is reflective of a broader customer base and a multiplicity of perspectives.

As globalization intensifies, the skills required for effective leadership and management are evolving. Emotional intelligence, cultural sensitivity, and the ability to think systemically are increasingly valued. For managers, proficiency in cross-cultural communication and virtual team management are becoming essential skills. Both leaders and managers must also become adept at change management, as the rate of change in the global business environment continues to accelerate.

Therefore, globalization is not merely an external trend that organizations must react to; it's a dynamic force that is actively reshaping the roles of leaders and managers. Those who can adapt to this evolving landscape are better positioned to guide their organizations toward success in the global arena, making the most of the opportunities it presents while mitigating its challenges.

Technological Advancements and Their Effects

As we advance further into the 21st century, technological advancements like Artificial Intelligence (AI), Big Data, and the Internet of Things (IoT) are having profound impacts on both leadership and management roles. These technologies are not just tools for automation or efficiency; they are catalysts that are significantly reshaping organizational paradigms and the nature of work itself.

Take AI, for example. Its role in decision-making processes can't be overstated. Where leaders once relied on instinct and experience to make strategic decisions, AI offers data-driven insights that can profoundly affect an organization's direction. This raises new questions about the role of human intuition and judgment, as leaders will increasingly need to harmonize their instincts with algorithmic recommendations. Managers too will see their roles transformed. AI can handle routine tasks, freeing managers to focus on more complex responsibilities such as employee development and strategic implementation. However, this also means that managers will need to understand how these algorithms work, to ensure they align with organizational goals and ethical considerations.

Big Data similarly has vast implications. The ability to collect and analyze enormous sets of data can be a game-changer in market analysis, customer engagement, and internal decision-making processes. Leaders will need to grasp the broader implications of Big Data, incorporating it into their vision for the organization's future. Managers will find themselves tasked with implementing data-driven strategies, requiring a familiarity with data analytics tools and techniques. The potential downside is the risk of "analysis paralysis," where the sheer volume of data overwhelms decision-making capabilities, making the roles of leaders and managers even more critical in synthesizing and acting upon data in a meaningful way.

The Internet of Things (IoT) adds another layer to this technological transformation. With devices constantly collecting data, organizations have unprecedented access to real-time information. This can be a boon for both leaders and managers, offering real-time insights into operational efficiencies, customer behavior, and market trends. However, this also requires a new level of technical literacy, as these leaders and managers will need to understand how to leverage IoT effectively.

Technological advancements are also likely to result in significant changes in team dynamics and organizational structures. The hierarchy-based model could give way to more fluid, project-based structures, enabled by technologies that allow for more distributed, yet still connected, working environments. Leadership in this landscape will require a focus on fostering a culture of continuous learning and adaptability. Management tasks will increasingly involve coordinating team efforts across a web of interconnected roles and responsibilities, many of which may be automated or data-driven.

In summary, technological advancements are not just shaping the future; they are actively transforming the roles and requirements of leadership and management. Adapting to this new landscape is not optional but essential for the success and sustainability of organizations in this digital age.

The Changing Nature of Work

The future of work is undergoing seismic shifts, influenced by factors such as the rise of remote work, freelancing, and the gig economy. These trends not only challenge traditional ideas about what a "workplace" is but also have significant implications for leadership and management roles.

The sudden adoption of remote work, accelerated by global events like the COVID-19 pandemic, has been a litmus test for both leaders and managers. Leaders have to find new ways to inspire teams, maintain a coherent organizational culture, and articulate a vision that resonates across digital platforms. Gone are the days when a leader's physical presence in an office setting was enough to exert influence and maintain authority. The skill set now includes digital proficiency, a mastery of remote communication tools, and an ability to build relationships in a virtual environment.

Similarly, managers overseeing remote teams face challenges that are different from those in an in-person setting. Remote work requires a shift from supervising to empowering, as micromanagement is not only less feasible but also less effective in a remote setting. Managers now need to be adept at setting clear expectations, using key performance indicators that are appropriate for remote work, and fostering a sense of accountability without the overhang of constant oversight.

The increase in freelancing and the gig economy complicates this dynamic even further. Traditional management approaches often depend on long-term relationships and in-depth understanding of team members, something that is not always possible when working with freelancers or short-term contractors. Managers must adapt their skills to include better upfront communication, clearly defined project scopes, and an ability to align short-term team members with the organization's broader objectives.

Leadership also needs to evolve in the gig economy landscape. One key challenge is how to engender a sense of loyalty and coherence among a constantly changing workforce. Here, a leader's role in building a strong, attractive organizational culture becomes even more critical. The focus shifts towards creating an environment where gig workers, freelancers, and permanent staff feel equally invested, even if their engagement with the organization differs in length and depth.

As teams become more diverse and geographically distributed, leaders and managers have to be increasingly sensitive to cross-cultural considerations. This adds layers of complexity to communication, team dynamics, and decision-making processes.

The changing nature of work calls for a new paradigm of leadership and management. It is a landscape where agility, emotional intelligence, digital proficiency, and a global mindset are no longer just buzzwords but essential competencies. Organizations that are quick to recognize and adapt to these changes are likely to be the ones that thrive in this new era of work.

Evolving Corporate Ethics and Social Responsibilities

The business landscape is also becoming increasingly attuned to issues of corporate social responsibility (CSR) and ethical governance. This is not just a fad or a nice-to-have, but an essential facet of modern business that has profound implications for both leadership and management roles.

Leaders are no longer judged solely on the basis of short-term profitability but are increasingly held accountable for the long-term impact of their decisions on society and the environment. This is a complex, multi-faceted role that involves balancing the interests of diverse stakeholders, including employees, customers, investors, and the broader community. It calls for ethical leadership that places importance on transparency, sustainability, and social justice. Business leaders are expected to embody these values in their strategic decisions, from choosing sustainable suppliers to implementing diversity and inclusion policies.

This shift towards more conscientious business practices also changes the game for managers. It is no longer sufficient to meet performance metrics in a vacuum. Managers are now expected to achieve goals within the framework of ethical considerations and social responsibilities. This could mean ensuring the fair treatment of employees, upholding data privacy standards, or managing resources in an environmentally friendly manner. Furthermore, managers have a crucial role in embedding these principles into the day-to-day operations of the company. They act as a conduit between the visionary ideals set forth by leadership and the practical realities of business operations.

The focus on CSR and ethics often means that companies are scrutinized more than ever before. In this digital age, any lapse in ethical conduct can be quickly exposed and can have lasting ramifications for the company's reputation. Hence, ethical conduct and social responsibility are not just moral imperatives but also business imperatives that require thoughtful input from both leaders and managers.

The alignment of corporate goals with ethical and social responsibility is not merely a top-down imposition from leaders. It should be woven into the fabric of the company culture, reflected in the KPIs set by managers, and instilled into the ethos of teams across the organization. This comprehensive approach ensures that the focus on doing good is not just a side project, but an integral part of how business is conducted.

Thus, the evolution in corporate ethics and social responsibilities brings new layers of complexity and nuance to the roles of leaders and managers alike. Organizations that are successful in integrating these elements will not only stand to gain in terms of reputation and customer loyalty but will also be better equipped to attract and retain top talent who are increasingly looking to work for companies that align with their own values.

Sustainability and Environmental Concerns

In a world grappling with climate change, resource depletion, and environmental degradation, sustainability has moved from the periphery to the center of organizational strategy. No longer is it just a buzzword or an appendage to the annual report; it's a critical factor that influences decision-making at all levels. This transformative emphasis on sustainability necessitates a corresponding shift in the roles and responsibilities of both leaders and managers.

Leaders are increasingly expected to be the champions of sustainability, driving the vision and strategic direction of the organization in a manner that is ecologically responsible. Their purview extends beyond the conventional metrics of profit and loss, encompassing a broader "triple bottom line" that considers social and environmental impacts. Leaders have the responsibility to foster partnerships with sustainable suppliers, make long-term investments in green technologies, and undertake initiatives that mitigate the organization's environmental footprint. This may also include lobbying for environmentally friendly policies and practices, not just within the organization, but also in the wider industry and community.

While leaders set the strategic course, it is the managers who must operationalize sustainability within the organization. The task of a manager has expanded to include overseeing the efficient use of resources, minimizing waste, and facilitating the adoption of sustainable technologies. This might manifest in very practical terms, such as optimizing supply chain logistics for lower carbon emissions, implementing recycling programs, or transitioning to renewable energy sources for operations. Moreover, managers have to keep their teams engaged and informed about sustainability goals, integrating these into performance metrics and day-to-day activities.

In this context, managers become the facilitators of sustainable practices. For example, if a company leader announces a commitment to become carbon-neutral by a certain date, managers are the ones who will break down this large strategic goal into actionable tasks. They will identify the specific changes needed in each department, procure the necessary resources, and implement monitoring systems to track progress.

Sustainability concerns may also require managers and leaders to collaborate more closely with a wider range of stakeholders, including community organizations, environmental experts, and even competitors. This multi-stakeholder approach often leads to more innovative and comprehensive solutions, but it also requires adept communication and negotiation skills.

The emphasis on sustainability is redefining what effective leadership and management look like, embedding ecological responsibility into the very DNA of these roles. Organizations that adapt to this new paradigm will not only contribute positively to environmental stewardship but are also likely to see benefits in terms of operational efficiencies, stakeholder relationships, and long-term viability.

Leadership and Management Education

The growing complexities of the business world, accelerated by factors such as globalization, technological advancements, and an increased focus on sustainability and ethics, have led to changes in what is expected of both leaders and managers. As a result, there's a palpable shift in educational curricula and training programs designed to develop the next generation of organizational leaders and managers.

Management education, often encapsulated within MBA programs, was primarily centered on teaching hard skills such as finance, marketing, and operations management. Leadership training, on the other hand, was often more ethereal, focused on qualities such as vision, inspiration, and charisma. However, contemporary programs are increasingly blending these two, acknowledging that a well-rounded executive should be both a competent manager and an inspiring leader. Courses on ethical governance, corporate social responsibility, and sustainability have become mainstays, reflecting the new areas where leadership and management are expected to have competence.

Soft skills like emotional intelligence, adaptability, and cross-cultural competency are gaining prominence in educational setups. These skills are essential for navigating the diverse, rapidly changing landscapes that modern organizations operate in. Simulation exercises, real-world case studies, and experiential learning opportunities are being integrated into curricula to provide hands-on experience and to help students understand the practical implications of their decisions.

The concept of lifelong learning has also taken on newfound importance in this era. The rate at which new technologies and methodologies are introduced has accelerated to the point that skills can become obsolete within a few years. Thus, the onus of staying relevant now falls both on the individual and the organization they belong to. Many companies are establishing ongoing training programs, offering opportunities for upskilling and reskilling to ensure that their employees stay current. These may range from workshops on the latest project management software to leadership training programs that focus on leading remote or culturally diverse teams.

Online courses, webinars, and certificate programs have also proliferated, offering easier access to continued education. In this digital age, the barriers to ongoing skill development have been significantly lowered, allowing for a more democratized access to educational resources. In fact, the stigma around online or alternative forms of education is quickly dissipating, as employers come to value the proactive commitment to personal and professional development that such efforts demonstrate.

The changes in the landscape of leadership and management are being mirrored in educational and training paradigms. The curricula are evolving to produce hybrid leader-managers equipped with a blend of hard and soft skills, technical acumen, and a deeply ingrained sense of ethics and sustainability. The focus is shifting from simply preparing students for the world as it is, to enabling them to lead and manage the organizations of the future effectively.

The Role of Women and Minorities in Leadership and Management

The dialogue surrounding the role of women and minorities in leadership and management positions is increasingly gaining momentum, fueled by both societal expectations and the recognition of the tangible benefits that come with diverse leadership. Despite progress, women and ethnic minorities are still underrepresented in top roles across various industries. However, there is a growing body of evidence that points to the financial and strategic advantages of having a diverse leadership team, leading to more efforts to balance representation.

Current trends show a slow yet consistent increase in the number of women and minorities occupying managerial and leadership positions. Many organizations have started to adopt diversity targets and are actively measuring and reporting their diversity metrics. Even venture capital firms and shareholders are starting to pressurize companies for greater diversity at the board and executive levels. Future projections suggest that if the current rate of change continues, we'll see a more balanced representation in the coming decades, although there's a consensus that the pace of change needs to accelerate.

Creating an environment that fosters diversity and inclusion goes beyond quotas or affirmative action. It begins with cultivating an organizational culture that values different perspectives and backgrounds. Bias training, mentorship programs tailored for underrepresented groups, and creating channels for reporting discriminatory behavior are a few methods that can be effective. However, it's crucial that these initiatives are not just 'box-checking' exercises but are deeply integrated into the company's values and long-term strategies. Organizations must also strive to remove systemic barriers that hinder the career progression of women and minorities. For instance, offering flexible working arrangements can make it easier for women to balance work with family obligations, thereby aiding in retention and progression.

Moreover, the role of leadership in fostering diversity cannot be overstated. Leaders need to be committed to diversity and should be held accountable for achieving diversity and inclusion goals. They have the power to set the tone for the organizational culture and can inspire change by setting an example. Companies where the leadership actively engages in diversity initiatives often see more significant improvement compared to when such initiatives are left to the human resources department alone.

In the future, as organizations become more global and connected, the ability to lead and manage diverse teams will become even more crucial. Gender and ethnic diversity will likely be joined by other dimensions of diversity, such as neurodiversity, and organizations will be expected to adapt and broaden their inclusion efforts accordingly.

The role of women and minorities in leadership and management is undergoing a transformative shift. There's an increasing awareness that diversity isn't just a moral obligation but also a business imperative. Organizations are taking various steps to foster diversity and inclusion, but a lot still needs to be done. The progress made in the upcoming years will be a telling indicator of how deeply these values are integrated into the fabric of organizational culture.

Preparing for Unpredictable Futures

As we move further into an age marked by rapid technological advancements, geopolitical shifts, and environmental uncertainties, the need for resilience and adaptability in leadership and management has never been more pronounced. The reality is that the business landscape is not just changing; it's becoming increasingly volatile and unpredictable. This calls for a new kind of preparedness, one that involves not just strategic foresight but also the ability to adapt and pivot quickly in response to unforeseen challenges.

Resilience is not just about bouncing back from setbacks; it's about bouncing forward. It involves not just recovery, but also learning and growth. For leaders and managers, resilience translates to the ability to maintain composure under stress, to learn from mistakes, and to use challenges as steppingstones rather than stumbling blocks. Companies that are resilient are better at crisis management, more adept at-risk mitigation, and more likely to emerge from challenging situations stronger than before.

Adaptability, too, is key. As the saying goes, "It is not the strongest of the species that survives, nor the most intelligent; it is the one most responsive to change." In a business context, adaptability involves everything from the willingness to adopt new technologies to the ability to change business models in response to market shifts. It involves a culture of continuous learning and improvement, where feedback is actively sought and used for growth.

Contingency planning is another vital area of focus. It involves preparing for various scenarios, including worst-case ones, and having plans in place to deal with them. In today's complex environment, traditional approaches to planning, built on the assumption of a stable and predictable future, are often insufficient. Scenario planning, which involves preparing for multiple, plausible future states, is becoming an increasingly important tool in the strategic planner's toolkit.

For professionals looking to prepare for these uncertainties, continuous learning is key. Whether it's keeping up with the latest advancements in your field, learning new skills, or expanding your knowledge base, the importance of being a lifelong learner cannot be overstated. Also critical is the need to build and maintain a strong professional network. In unpredictable times, a robust network can serve as a valuable resource, providing support, advice, and even job opportunities. Emotional intelligence, including skills like empathy, self-awareness, and effective communication, is another critical area for development. In an uncertain world, the ability to manage not just one's own emotions but also to understand and influence the emotions of others can be a significant asset.

As we look towards the future, it is clear that the skills and attributes that will be most valued in leaders and managers are evolving. With unpredictability as the new normal, resilience, adaptability, and effective contingency planning are not just desirable traits; they are essential. Professionals can prepare for this uncertain future by investing in continuous learning, by building strong networks, and by developing their emotional intelligence. This preparedness won't just make them more effective in their roles; it will also make them more valuable contributors to their organizations, better able to navigate the complexities and challenges that lie ahead.

Final Thoughts and Summary Conclusion

In this concluding chapter, we've journeyed through the transformative influences that are shaping the future of leadership and management. From globalization's far-reaching implications to the cutting-edge technologies that are disrupting traditional organizational hierarchies, it's evident that the roles of both leaders and managers are in a state of flux. The increasing focus on corporate ethics and social responsibilities, the evolving landscape of work, and the urgent calls for sustainability all signify that a dynamic skill set is now the minimum requirement for success. As these trends gain momentum, their impact on organizations and professionals will only intensify.

But while the future is fraught with challenges, it is also ripe with opportunities for those willing to adapt and evolve. The best leaders and managers of tomorrow will be those who view change not as a threat but as an invitation to innovate and improve. They will be individuals who are committed to lifelong learning and who are proactive about broadening their knowledge and skills. With the world changing at an unprecedented pace, flexibility, adaptability, and a forward-thinking mindset will be more crucial than ever.

Embracing change requires a departure from the comfort zone—it calls for the courage to confront uncertainties and the openness to learn from both successes and failures. But those who make this choice, who commit to continuous adaptation and growth, will not only survive the changes; they will thrive in them. They will be the ones to forge new paths in uncharted territories, to set new standards of excellence, and to lead their organizations into the future.

So, as we wrap up this comprehensive exploration of leadership and management, let's embrace the complexities and uncertainties of the present age as the catalysts that they are. Let them spur us on to new heights of innovation, compel us to deepen our understanding, and inspire us to become the best versions of ourselves. For in a world that is constantly changing, the one constant is our ability to change with it. Here's to your journey of continuous adaptation, growth, and success.

References

Introduction

Bass, B. M. (1985). Leadership and Performance Beyond Expectations. New York: Free Press.

Collins, J. (2001). Good to Great: Why Some Companies Make the Leap... and Others Don't. HarperCollins.

Drucker, P. F. (2008). Management: Tasks, Responsibilities, Practices. HarperCollins.

Goleman, D. (1998). Working with Emotional Intelligence. New York: Bantam Books.

Heifetz, R. A., Grashow, A., & Linsky, M. (2009). The Practice of Adaptive Leadership: Tools and Tactics for Changing Your Organization and the World. Harvard Business Press.

Hersey, P., Blanchard, K. H., & Johnson, D. E. (2008). Management of Organizational Behavior: Leading Human Resources (9th ed.). Prentice Hall.

Kotter, J. P. (1996). Leading Change. Boston: Harvard Business School Press.

Mintzberg, H. (1973). The Nature of Managerial Work. Harper & Row.

Northouse, P. G. (2018). Leadership: Theory and Practice (8th ed.). Sage Publications.

Pink, D. H. (2009). Drive: The Surprising Truth About What Motivates Us. Riverhead Books.

Schein, E. H. (2016). Organizational Culture and Leadership (5th ed.). Wiley.

Senge, P. M. (1990). The Fifth Discipline: The Art & Practice of The Learning Organization. Doubleday.

Yukl, G. (2012). Leadership in Organizations (8th ed.). Pearson.

Chapter 1

Avolio, B. J., & Bass, B. M. (1995). Multifactor Leadership Questionnaire. Mind Garden, Inc.

Bennis, W. (1989). On Becoming a Leader. Addison-Wesley.

Blanchard, K. H., & Hersey, P. (1996). Management of Organizational Behavior: Utilizing Human Resources (6th ed.). Prentice Hall.

Burns, J. M. (1978). Leadership. Harper & Row.

Covey, S. R. (1989). The Seven Habits of Highly Effective People. Free Press.

Daft, R. L. (2014). The Leadership Experience (6th ed.). Cengage Learning.

Fiedler, F. E. (1967). A Theory of Leadership Effectiveness. McGraw-Hill.

Greenleaf, R. K. (1977). Servant Leadership: A Journey into the Nature of Legitimate Power and Greatness. Paulist Press.

Hackman, J. R., & Wageman, R. (2005). A Theory of Team Coaching. Academy of Management Review, 30(2), 269-287.

HBR's 10 Must Reads on Leadership (2011). Harvard Business Review Press.

Lencioni, P. (2002). The Five Dysfunctions of a Team: A Leadership Fable. Jossey-Bass.

Maxwell, J. C. (1993). Developing the Leader Within You. Thomas Nelson.

Robbins, S. P., & Coulter, M. (2016). Management (13th ed.). Pearson.

Tichy, N. M., & Devanna, M. A. (1986). The Transformational Leader. John Wiley & Sons.

Zaleznik, A. (1977). Managers and Leaders: Are They Different? Harvard Business Review, 55(5), 67-78.

Chapter 2

Adair, J. (1988). Effective Leadership. Pan Macmillan.

Bass, B. M., & Riggio, R. E. (2006). Transformational Leadership (2nd ed.). Psychology Press.

Collins, J. (2001). Good to Great. HarperBusiness.

Drucker, P. F. (1999). Management Challenges for the 21st Century. HarperBusiness.

Goleman, D. (1998). Working with Emotional Intelligence. Bantam Books.

Hersey, P., Blanchard, K. H., & Johnson, D. E. (1996). Management of Organizational Behavior: Leading Human Resources (7th ed.). Prentice Hall.

Katzenbach, J. R., & Smith, D. K. (1993). The Wisdom of Teams. Harvard Business School Press.

Kouzes, J. M., & Posner, B. Z. (1987). The Leadership Challenge. Jossey-Bass.

Locke, E. A. (1991). Goal Setting: A Motivational Technique That Works!. Prentice Hall.

Mintzberg, H. (1973). The Nature of Managerial Work. Harper & Row.

Pink, D. H. (2009). Drive: The Surprising Truth About What Motivates Us. Riverhead Books.

Porter, M. E. (1980). Competitive Strategy. Free Press.

Sinek, S. (2009). Start with Why. Penguin Books.

Taylor, F. W. (1911). The Principles of Scientific Management. Harper & Brothers.

Tuckman, B. W. (1965). Developmental sequence in small groups. Psychological Bulletin, 63(6), 384-399.

Chapter 3

Argyris, C. (1999). On Organizational Learning (2nd ed.). Blackwell Publishing.

Covey, S. R. (1989). The 7 Habits of Highly Effective People. Free Press.

Csikszentmihalyi, M. (1990). Flow: The Psychology of Optimal Experience. Harper & Row.

Fiedler, F. E. (1967). A Theory of Leadership Effectiveness. McGraw-Hill.

Gladwell, M. (2000). The Tipping Point: How Little Things Can Make a Big Difference. Little, Brown and Company.

Hackman, J. R. (2002). Leading Teams: Setting the Stage for Great Performances. Harvard Business School Press.

Heifetz, R. A. (1994). Leadership Without Easy Answers. Harvard University Press.

Kotter, J. P. (1996). Leading Change. Harvard Business School Press.

Lewin, K. (1947). Frontiers in group dynamics. Human Relations, 1(1), 5-41.

McGregor, D. (1960). The Human Side of Enterprise. McGraw-Hill.

Senge, P. M. (1990). The Fifth Discipline. Doubleday/Currency.
Vroom, V. H., & Yetton, P. W. (1973). Leadership and Decision-making. University of Pittsburgh Press.

Chapter 4

Blake, R. R., & Mouton, J. S. (1964). The Managerial Grid: Key Orientations for Achieving Production through People. Gulf Publishing Co.

Bolman, L. G., & Deal, T. E. (2017). Reframing Organizations: Artistry, Choice, and Leadership (6th ed.). Jossey-Bass.

Collins, J. (2001). Good to Great: Why Some Companies Make the Leap and Others Don't. HarperBusiness.

Drucker, P. (1954). The Practice of Management. Harper & Row.

Goleman, D. (1998). Working with Emotional Intelligence. Bantam Books.

Hersey, P., & Blanchard, K. H. (1969). Life Cycle Theory of Leadership. Training and Development Journal.

Herzberg, F. (1968). One More Time: How Do You Motivate Employees?. Harvard Business Review.

House, R. J. (1971). A Path-Goal Theory of Leader Effectiveness. Administrative Science Quarterly.

Kouzes, J. M., & Posner, B. Z. (1987). The Leadership Challenge. Jossey-Bass.

Mintzberg, H. (1973). The Nature of Managerial Work. Harper & Row.

Northouse, P. G. (2018). Leadership: Theory and Practice (8th ed.). SAGE Publications.

Pink, D. H. (2009). Drive: The Surprising Truth About What Motivates Us. Riverhead Books.

Porter, M. E. (1985). Competitive Advantage. Free Press.

Schein, E. H. (2010). Organizational Culture and Leadership (4th ed.). Jossey-Bass.

Taylor, F. W. (1911). The Principles of Scientific Management. Harper & Brothers.

Tuckman, B. W. (1965). Developmental sequence in small groups. Psychological Bulletin, 63, 384–399.

Chapter 5

Adair, J. (1983). Effective Leadership: A Modern Guide to Developing Leadership Skills. Pan Books.

Bennis, W. (1989). On Becoming a Leader. Addison-Wesley.

Covey, S. R. (1989). The Seven Habits of Highly Effective People. Free Press.

Drath, W. H., & Palus, C. J. (1994). Making Common Sense: Leadership as Meaning-Making in a Community of Practice. Center for Creative Leadership.

Fiedler, F. E. (1967). A Theory of Leadership Effectiveness. McGraw-Hill.

Greenleaf, R. K. (1977). Servant Leadership: A Journey into the Nature of Legitimate Power and Greatness. Paulist Press.

Heifetz, R. A., & Linsky, M. (2002). Leadership on the Line: Staying Alive through the Dangers of Leading. Harvard Business School Press.

Kotter, J. P. (1990). A Force for Change: How Leadership Differs from Management. Free Press.

Lewin, K., Lippitt, R., & White, R. K. (1939). Patterns of aggressive behavior in experimentally created "social climates". Journal of Social Psychology.

Mayo, E. (1945). The Social Problems of an Industrial Civilization. Routledge.

McGregor, D. (1960). The Human Side of Enterprise. McGraw-Hill.

Senge, P. M. (1990). The Fifth Discipline: The Art & Practice of The Learning Organization. Doubleday/Currency.

Vroom, V. H., & Yetton, P. W. (1973). Leadership and Decision-Making. University of Pittsburgh Press.

Yukl, G. (2012). Leadership in Organizations (8th ed.). Pearson.

Chapter 6

Avolio, B. J., Walumbwa, F. O., & Weber, T. J. (2009). Leadership: Current Theories, Research, and Future Directions. Annual Review of Psychology.

Bass, B. M., & Stogdill, R. M. (1990). Bass & Stogdill's Handbook of Leadership: Theory, Research, and Managerial Applications. Free Press.

Blanchard, K. H., & Hersey, P. (1969). Management of Organizational Behavior. Prentice Hall.

Collins, J. (2001). Good to Great: Why Some Companies Make the Leap...and Others Don't. HarperBusiness.

Conger, J. A., & Kanungo, R. N. (1988). Charismatic Leadership: The Elusive Factor in Organizational Effectiveness. Jossey-Bass.

Goleman, D., Boyatzis, R., & McKee, A. (2002). Primal Leadership: Realizing the Power of Emotional Intelligence. Harvard Business School Press.

Hackman, J. R., & Wageman, R. (2007). Asking the Right Questions About Leadership. American Psychologist.
House, R. J., & Aditya, R. N. (1997). The Social Scientific Study of Leadership: Quo Vadis?. Journal of Management.

Hughes, R. L., Ginnett, R. C., & Curphy, G. J. (1993). Leadership: Enhancing the Lessons of Experience. Irwin.

Kotter, J. P. (1995). Leading Change: Why Transformation Efforts Fail. Harvard Business Review.

Kouzes, J. M., & Posner, B. Z. (1987). The Leadership Challenge. Jossey-Bass.

Mintzberg, H. (1973). The Nature of Managerial Work. Harper & Row.

Northouse, P. G. (2018). Leadership: Theory and Practice (8th ed.). Sage Publications.

O'Toole, J. (1996). Leading Change: Overcoming the Ideology of Comfort and the Tyranny of Custom. Jossey-Bass.

Rost, J. C. (1993). Leadership for the Twenty-First Century. Praeger.

Schein, E. H. (2010). Organizational Culture and Leadership. Jossey-Bass.

Sinek, S. (2009). Start with Why: How Great Leaders Inspire Everyone to Take Action. Portfolio.

Tichy, N. M., & Devanna, M. A. (1986). The Transformational Leader. John Wiley & Sons.

Zenger, J., & Folkman, J. (2002). The Extraordinary Leader: Turning Good Managers into Great Leaders. McGraw-Hill.

Chapter 7

Bennis, W. (1989). On Becoming a Leader. Addison-Wesley.

Drucker, P. (2008). Management: Tasks, Responsibilities, Practices. Harper & Row.

Finkelstein, S., & Hambrick, D. C. (1996). Strategic Leadership: Top Executives and Their Effects on Organizations. West Publishing Company.

Goffee, R., & Jones, G. (2006). Why Should Anyone Be Led by You?. Harvard Business Review Press.

Heifetz, R. A. (1994). Leadership Without Easy Answers. Belknap Press.

Hersey, P., & Blanchard, K. H. (1988). Management of Organizational Behavior: Utilizing Human Resources. Prentice-Hall.

Huy, Q. N. (2001). In Praise of Middle Managers. Harvard Business Review.

Ibarra, H. (2015). Act Like a Leader, Think Like a Leader. Harvard Business Review Press.

Kotter, J. P. (2001). What Leaders Really Do. Harvard Business Review Press.

Lencioni, P. (2002). The Five Dysfunctions of a Team: A Leadership Fable. Jossey-Bass.

Yukl, G. (2012). Leadership in Organizations (8th ed.). Pearson.

Chapter 8

Brynjolfsson, E., & McAfee, A. (2014). The Second Machine Age: Work, Progress, and Prosperity in a Time of Brilliant Technologies. W. W. Norton & Company.

Christensen, C. M., & Overdorf, M. (2000). Meeting the Challenge of Disruptive Change. Harvard Business Review.

Collins, J., & Hansen, M. T. (2011). Great by Choice. Harper Business.

Drucker, P. (1999). Management Challenges for the 21st Century. HarperCollins.

Duhigg, C. (2016). Smarter Faster Better: The Transformative Power of Real Productivity. Random House.

Friedman, T. L. (2016). Thank You for Being Late: An Optimist's Guide to Thriving in the Age of Accelerations. Farrar, Straus and Giroux.

Kim, G., Humble, J., Debois, P., & Willis, J. (2016). The DevOps Handbook: How to Create World-Class Agility, Reliability, & Security in Technology Organizations. IT Revolution Press.

McAfee, A., & Brynjolfsson, E. (2017). Machine, Platform, Crowd: Harnessing Our Digital Future. W. W. Norton & Company.

Porter, M. E., & Heppelmann, J. E. (2014). How Smart, Connected Products Are Transforming Competition. Harvard Business Review.

Ross, J. W., & Beath, C. M. (2017). Designed for Digital: How to Architect Your Business for Sustained Success. MIT Press.

Satell, G. (2017). Mapping Innovation: A Playbook for Navigating a Disruptive Age. McGraw-Hill Education.

Schwab, K. (2016). The Fourth Industrial Revolution. World Economic Forum.

Sinek, S. (2019). The Infinite Game. Portfolio.

Tapscott, D., & Tapscott, A. (2016). Blockchain Revolution: How the Technology Behind Bitcoin and Other Cryptocurrencies is Changing the World. Penguin Books.

Toffler, A. (1980). The Third Wave. William Morrow and Company.

Westerman, G., Bonnet, D., & McAfee, A. (2014). Leading Digital: Turning Technology into Business Transformation. Harvard Business Review Press.

Chapter 9

Bennis, W. (1989). On Becoming a Leader. Basic Books.

Bolman, L. G., & Deal, T. E. (2017). Reframing Organizations: Artistry, Choice, and Leadership. Jossey-Bass.

Collins, J. (2001). Good to Great: Why Some Companies Make the Leap... and Others Don't. HarperCollins Publishers.

Drucker, P. F. (2008). Management Cases. HarperCollins.
Finkelstein, S., & Sanford, S. H. (2003). Why Smart Executives Fail: And What You Can Learn from Their Mistakes. Portfolio.

Gladwell, M. (2008). Outliers: The Story of Success. Little, Brown and Co.
Hamel, G. (2000). Leading the Revolution. Harvard Business School Press.

Heifetz, R. A., Grashow, A., & Linsky, M. (2009). The Practice of Adaptive Leadership: Tools and Tactics for Changing Your Organization and the World. Harvard Business Review Press.

Kotter, J. P. (1996). Leading Change. Harvard Business Review Press.

Mintzberg, H. (1973). The Nature of Managerial Work. Harper & Row.

Pfeffer, J., & Sutton, R. I. (2006). Hard Facts, Dangerous Half-Truths, and Total Nonsense: Profiting from Evidence-Based Management. Harvard Business School Press.

Scharmer, C. O., & Kaufer, K. (2013). Leading from the Emerging Future: From Ego-System to Eco-System Economies. Berrett-Koehler Publishers.

Senge, P. M. (1990). The Fifth Discipline: The Art & Practice of the Learning Organization. Currency Doubleday.

Zenger, J., & Folkman, J. (2002). The Extraordinary Leader: Turning Good Managers into Great Leaders. McGraw-Hill.

Conclusion

Brynjolfsson, E., & McAfee, A. (2014). The Second Machine Age: Work, Progress, and Prosperity in a Time of Brilliant Technologies. W. W. Norton & Company.

Christensen, C. M., Hall, T., Dillon, K., & Duncan, D. S. (2016). Competing Against Luck: The Story of Innovation and Customer Choice. Harper Business.
Drucker, P. F. (1999). Management Challenges for the 21st Century. HarperBusiness.

Friedman, T. L. (2016). Thank You for Being Late: An Optimist's Guide to Thriving in the Age of Accelerations. Farrar, Straus and Giroux.

Harari, Y. N. (2018). 21 Lessons for the 21st Century. Spiegel & Grau.

Sinek, S. (2019). The Infinite Game. Portfolio/Penguin.
Tapscott, D., & Tapscott, A. (2016). Blockchain Revolution: How the Technology Behind Bitcoin and Other Cryptocurrencies is Changing the World. Portfolio.